DISCARDED

PROFILES IN AMERICAN FOREIGN POLICY:

STIMSON, KENNAN, ACHESON,
DULLES, RUSK, KISSINGER, AND VANCE

Peter A. Poole

Illustrations by
John Perts

University Press
of America

Copyright © 1981 by
University Press of America, Inc.™
P.O. Box 19101, Washington, D.C. 20036

All rights reserved

Printed in the United States of America

ISBN: 0-8191-1423-5 (Perfect)
0-8191-1422-7 (Cloth)

Library of Congress Number: 80-5624

Illustrations copyright © 1981 by
John Perts

PREFACE

This book offers profiles of seven leaders of American foreign policy, four of whom served during the years of United States military and economic dominance in the 1940s and 1950s. They are: Henry Stimson, George Kennan, Dean Acheson, and John Foster Dulles. The last three members of the succession, Dean Rusk, Henry Kissinger, and Cyrus Vance presided over our country's painful readjustment to the status of a "normal great power." The American foreign policy tradition has been enormously influenced by the contributions of these statesmen. Whether one agrees or disagrees with their positions, it is important for the student and the general reader to be aware of the role they played in shaping the choices we now have before us.

I find I have been gathering material for this book for more than twenty years. Shortly after becoming a Foreign Service Officer in 1959, I was assigned to the American Embassy in Cambodia. One of the highlights of that tour was serving as escort officer to Mr. and Mrs. Acheson during their 1962 visit. Dean Acheson later talked with me about the events in Chapter 4 at his home in Washington.

Service in Thailand followed, during which I completed my dissertation. While teaching at Howard University, from 1969 to 1972, I began a series of interviews with major figures in U.S. foreign policy. As noted in the text, Dean Rusk and George Kennan were among those who kindly granted me some of their time to discuss the episodes in Chapters 3 and 6. Dean Rusk granted me a subsequent interview in April 1980.

I also wish to thank the following officials and former officials for taking time to enrich my understanding of the subjects of these profiles: the late John M. Allison, Robert W. Barnett, McGeorge Bundy, William P. Bundy, W. Walton Butterworth, J. William Fulbright, Marshall Green, Averell Harriman, Roger Hilsman, J. Graham Parsons, Edwin O. Reischauer, the late Walter Robertson, John Service, Philip D. Sprouse, William H. Sullivan, James C. Thomson, Jr., William C. Trimble, and the late John Carter Vincent.

From 1975 to 1977, I served as Senator Charles Percy's legislative assistant on the Foreign Relations Committee. From that vantage point, I was able to attend many of the hearings at which Secretary Henry Kissinger testified. I thus had a valuable opportunity to experience the atmosphere in Congress during that period of intense struggle with the executive branch.

I also wish to thank my students and colleagues at Old Dominion University since 1977 for stimulating and responding to many of the ideas expressed in these profiles. I am grateful to the Research Foundation of Old Dominion University and to the School of Arts and Letters for grants that have made it possible to complete this volume. My thanks also to Evangeline Buggs and Carole Johnson, who typed several drafts of the manuscript.

This book is dedicated to David and Alice Spangler, whose home in Washington my wife and I have often visited. Our friendship goes back many years to when we were all assigned in Cambodia--in much happier days for that country.

My wife, Rosemary Poole, has contributed sound editorial advice which improved the substance and style of the manuscript.

Sugar Hill, N.H.   PETER A. POOLE
and Norfolk, VA.

TABLE OF CONTENTS

Preface. ii

Chapter

1. THE SUCCESSION OF AMERICAN
   FOREIGN POLICY LEADERS.   1

2. HENRY STIMSON AND THE EXPANDED
   PRESIDENCY.   9

3. GEORGE KENNAN: AUTHOR AND CRITIC
   OF THE CONTAINMENT POLICY 25

4. DEAN ACHESON: THE SEARCH FOR WORLD
   ORDER 45

5. JOHN FOSTER DULLES: HARD-LINER
   OR TIGHTROPE-WALKER?. 65

6. DEAN RUSK: CONTAINING COMMUNISM
   IN ASIA 81

7. KISSINGER AND INDOCHINA 99

8. CYRUS VANCE: FOCUS ON THE THIRD
   WORLD 115

SUGGESTIONS FOR READING. 135

Chapter 1

THE SUCCESSION OF AMERICAN

FOREIGN POLICY LEADERS

Our story begins in the late 1930s, in an atmosphere of global crisis. In Manchuria, Ethiopia, and Czechoslovakia, the Axis powers defied the shallow-rooted treaty system put in place by the victors in World War I. America remained, as it had been since the turn of the century, one of the great unknowns in world affairs. It could be a decisive factor when guided by skilled amateur diplomats such as Theodore Roosevelt. However, his successors often promised far more--or far less--than they could deliver.

For example, our leaders in the interwar period denied major power status to Japan and censured her moves in China--but U.S. interests in Asia were frequently described as not worth fighting for. This contradictory behavior invited war with Japan, though most of Roosevelt's advisers agreed by 1939 that Nazi Germany was the prime threat to Western interests.

The men who were destined to shape our foreign policy from 1940 to 1980 were deeply conscious of these past failures of American leadership. In the profiles that follow, we will encounter a succession of leaders whose collective view of the world was shaped by the Munich tragedy and by the later perception that Hitler's defeat made Stalin a dangerous enemy of the West. Each of the seven subscribed to the realist doctrine, in which military power sets the hierarchy among nations and tends to resolve even non-military issues. Likewise, they believed that strong presidential leadership was essential if the United States were to succeed in laying a new foundation for world order.

Henry Stimson was the bearer of the realist tradition from one Roosevelt administration to the next. He had been TR's U.S. Attorney in New York and Secretary of War under Taft. His second appointment as Secretary of War, in 1940, heralded America's entry into World War II. Stimson was close to each of the war-related decisions--particularly the concept of peacetime conscription--which greatly expanded the powers of the presidency in the early 1940s. He also took part in the early stages of reassessment of U.S.-Soviet relations. He advised President Truman to use the atomic bomb against Japan partly to show Stalin its effectiveness.

It was George Kennan, however, who first formulated the view that America must underwrite the recovery of Europe's war-weakened societies in order to "contain" Soviet Communism. During 1946, Kennan's predictions about Stalin's opportunistic behavior were confirmed by events in countries all around the Soviet Union, from Poland and Germany to Iran and Turkey. Kennan was recalled to Washington from the American Embassy in Moscow, and he played a major role in shaping U.S. policy in the reconstruction of Europe.

In the early postwar years, Kennan saw himself as helping to redress a pro-Moscow bias that had crept into American policy during the Second World War. However, he soon found that his concept of "containment" was being transformed into a militarist strategy of ringing Russia (and then China) with forward U.S. bases. Kennan tried to prevent this from happening to the U.S. posture in Asia. When he found that his influence was waning, he resigned from the State Department in 1950.

Dean Acheson was closely identified with the creation of the Bretton Woods system of world economic growth in worldwide trade and economic production. As Undersecretary of State, he played a key role in transforming the piecemeal U.S. response to the problems of a war-weakened Europe into the Truman Doctrine and Marshall Plan. He also supported a great increase in executive branch power--the unified Defense Department, the National Security Council, and the CIA.

After Truman named him Secretary of State in 1949, Acheson was forced to deal mainly with the Korean War and related Asian problems. These interested him less than Europe, and he found his freedom of action tightly constrained by Congressional critics. The main foreign policy accomplishment of Truman's second administration was the Japanese Peace Treaty. This allowed Japan to resume her full sovereignty and to become the world's first unarmed economic superpower. Acheson must share credit for this achievement with his special assistant and successor, John Foster Dulles, who negotiated the treaty.

As a leading foreign policy spokesman for the Republican moderate wing, Dulles helped build bipartisan support for U.S. policy during the Truman years. As Secretary of State, he completed a task he had begun along with the Japanese Peace Treaty in 1950; he negotiated a series of military agreements linking the United States to almost every non-Communist regime in Asia. His aim was to isolate and "contain" the Peoples Republic of China; the cost was a series of open-ended commitments.

In the early 1950s, Dulles adopted the public role of an anti-communist ideologue. He found this useful in dealing with Congress, and it also helped him control the headstrong leaders of our new Asian client states--Chiang Kai-shek, Ngo Dinh Diem, and Syngman Rhee. Dulles was able to persuade these proud leaders to moderate their views because they considered him their strongest supporter in Washington.

Elsewhere in the world, Dulles's highly personal and sometimes deceptive diplomacy met with less success. Perhaps his gravest disaster was the 1956 Suez crisis, in which he completely failed to communicate with our close allies, Britain, France and Israel; worst of all, the United States sided with Russia in a UN vote against its allies.

    Dulles's posturing as an anti-communist ideologue makes it hard to know how he might have adjusted--given a few more years of life--to the era when new power centers began to emerge. He died just as Japan and Western Europe completed their recovery and as the Sino-Soviet split broke into the open. As he battled the growing pain of cancer, Dulles seemed also to harden his own defenses against making any change in his foreign policy. While Eisenhower met with Khrushchev on terms of equality, Dulles thought it essential to stress America's military and moral superiority.

    Dean Rusk and John Foster Dulles had worked together in the early Korean War years to create a new bipartisan consensus on anti-communism in Asia. Ten years later, Rusk was named Secretary of State by a young, charismatic president who was determined to emphasize the contrast between himself and John Foster Dulles. Did John F. Kennedy realize just how closely Rusk had worked with Dulles in shaping the China containment policy?

    Only weeks after taking office, Kennedy's presidency suffered a major blow--the Bay of Pigs fiasco. For this ill-conceived and ill-advised aventure, Rusk and Robert McNamara must share the blame with the heads of the CIA and Joint Chiefs of Staff. However, this was only one of many symptoms of the collapse of strong, centralized control over our foreign affairs that followed Dulles's death. The free-wheeling CIA operations which began in 1959 were not fully checked even after the Bay of Pigs. The

4

assassination of Ngo Dinh Diem in 1963 was against the wishes of many of Kennedy's top advisors, including Rusk in particular.

President Kennedy had tried to balance the hawks and doves in the executive branch--giving the hawks a tougher posture in Vietnam after allowing Averell Harriman to "neutralize" Laos. Rusk had permitted McNamara to take the lead in shaping administration policy in Vietnam. Rusk sought to play a behind-the-scenes role as moderator between those in the Pentagon who favored a knock-out blow at Hanoi and those in the White House and State Department who wanted a Laotian-type solution. Unfortunately, the compromise policy of gradual escalation that resulted was no more feasible than either of the approaches that were seen at the time as "extremes."

During the Johnson years, Rusk and the President tried to adhere to the concept of a middle course--until half a million U.S. troops were committed with no sign of any increased political strength in Saigon. Despite all their combined knowledge of how Washington operates, neither Rusk nor Johnson had much interest in the politics of Southeast Asia. When Dean Acheson and other elder statesmen were asked for their views in 1968, they saw no possible alternative to withdrawing with minimum sacrifice of U.S. interests.

On entering the White House in 1969, Richard Nixon and his national security advisor, Henry Kissinger, set in motion a long overdue "era of negotiation." Nixon's reputation as an arch enemy of communism protected him from attacks on his political right. During his first term, he was also generally immune from attack by Senate liberals--first because he seemed to be winding down the war and secondly because American boys were still in the combat zone. Whatever individual Senators thought of "Vietnamization," they tended to believe the process was linked to Nixon's opening of a "dialogue" with China and Russia. The impression of a well-coordinated advance on all foreign policy fronts was cultivated by Kissinger, who became the idol of the media.

As soon as the 1973 Paris agreement was signed, however, Congress began to dissect Nixon's personal prestige and then the substance of his foreign policy. During 1975, the two branches of government were in continual conflict, beginning with the Indochina debacle and ending with the Senate's veto of aid to Angola. In this difficult period, Kissinger abandoned all pretense of following a carefully drawn conceptual blueprint; instead, he showed himself to be a masterful improviser.

Cyrus Vance, like many of his predecessors, was a corporation lawyer by training. He was given important diplomatic assignments during the Johnson years, and he earned respect as an effective, behind-the-scenes negotiator. During this three years as Secretary of State, he sought and often gained Congressional support for a policy of improving U.S. relations with the Third World. His record of achievement includes the Panama Canal Treaty, the Camp David Accords on the Middle East, full diplomatic relations with Peking, and substantial progress toward majority rule in Zimbabwe and Namibia.

Yet Vance faced a constant problem of making his voice heard over those of rival foreign policy advisors within the Carter administration. In particular, the president's national security advisor, Zbigniew Brzezinski, often succeeded in upstaging Secretary Vance by placing more emphasis on U.S.-Soviet rivalry than Vance thought necessary.

In early 1980, President Carter rejected Vance's advice against sending a U.S. commando team to rescue the American hostages in Iran. Vance became one of the few senior officials in American history to resign over an issue of foreign policy. His resignation focused attention on the fact that the national security advisor had grown into a rival secretary of state during the 1960s and 1970s. Future presidents might face unwelcome resistence--in the Senate, in the media, and on the part of their nominees as secretaries of state--if they continued to allow American foreign policy to be shaped and expounded by a White House aide who had not been confirmed by the Senate.

Vance's address to the 1980 Harvard Commencement was welcomed by many Americans for the clarity and sweep of vision which it offered. Thus, in the final chapter of this volume, we offer the full text of Mr. Vance's speech.

Henry Lewis Stimson

Chapter 2

HENRY STIMSON AND THE EXPANDED PRESIDENCY

In September 1945, Secretary of War Henry Stimson retired from his last governmental post with the full military pomp and circumstance that he loved. In the General Officers Mess at the Pentagon, he was given a huge birthday cake to mark his seventy-eighth birthday. At the cabinet meeting which followed, President Truman decorated him with the Distinguished Service Medal for his wartime contributions "from the beginning of the actual mobilization of the Army to the final victory over Japan." Then when he and Mrs. Stimson arrived at National Airport to begin their journey home, they found every general officer in Washington lined up in two long rows to say good-bye to their chief.

This stately, erect, domineering figure was a monument to the concept of "peace through military strength." He had served nearly every President since Theodore Roosevelt. Directly or indirectly, he touched the lives and careers of many American leaders of the cold war period. He more than anyone could say that he was "present at the creation" of the expanded presidency. He would have had no qualms about it.

Although he never managed to gain electoral office, Stimson's character and career earned him frequent comparisons with Winston Churchill. Each received the Spartan education by which Victorians of the upper class prepared their sons to manage empires.[1] Each of them also romanticized war and the life of a soldier. Stimson's first taste of battle came late in life, when he was nearly fifty, but he gloried in the few weeks he spent at the front in World War I. He always claimed to have ordered the first American artillery barrage of the war.

Stimson had already achieved prominence in public life before the war. Theodore Roosevelt, his friend and Long Island neighbor, had named him to the trust-busting post of U.S. Attorney for the second district of New York. Stimson fully approved of his chief's activism in foreign and domestic affairs and the great increase in the powers of the presidency during TR's administration. President Taft invited him to be Secretary of War, and he reorganized the sleepy little department.

Always a champion of Anglo-American unity, Stimson campaigned vigorously for America's entry into the war. Like Churchill, he became a major spokesman for military preparedness during the 1920s and thirties. They were also alike in their staunch defense of capitalism. Despite his trust-busting past, Stimson earned a fortune as a lawyer fighting the legal battles of private corporations.

During the interwar years, even in Coolidge's lackluster administration, Stimson found ways to pursue an activist approach to foreign affairs. He was sent to Nicaragua to help mediate a growing civil war. On his own initiative, he threatened U.S. naval reprisals if an insurgent force refused to lay down its arms. The "Peace of Tipitapa" which resulted from this threat lasted only a week but Stimson claimed to have demonstrated America's commitment to peace and order along the approaches to the Panama Canal.

Stimson also served as Governor of the Philippines during the 1920s, relishing the proconsular style that went with the office. He believed that America should never relinquish control of the islands, and he set himself the task of countering Filipino nationalism, to which Wilson and a Democratic Congress had catered. Stimson governed well and coopted the most able Filipino politicians into his cabinet.

After some hesitation, President Hoover named Stimson Secretary of State in 1929. The Quaker president and Stimson differed profoundly on the proper role of force in world affairs. Even so, they worked together to remove the friction in Anglo-American relations that had developed during the Coolidge years. Yet they were soon overwhelmed by the worldwide depression which undermined the treaty system on which world order depended.

The greatest single challenge Stimson faced, as Secretary of State, was Japan's occupation of Manchuria. Although, technically the region belonged to China, Japan had gradually asserted her economic, military, and political influence. When Stimson was sure the Tokyo government supported the takeover in "Manchukuo," he persuaded Hoover to announce that he would not recognize the puppet regime. Stimson argued that the Kellogg-Briand pact had outlawed war and licensed the United States (and other signatories) to use economic sanctions to punish those whom they considered agressors.

Hoover approved the nonrecognition policy-- but with the understanding that this was as far as he would go in punishing Japan. Stimson wanted to go much further and make nonrecognition merely the first step in a program of graduated pressures against Japan. This policy became known as the Stimson doctrine.

In the months before Roosevelt's inauguration, Stimson (though still serving Hoover) cultivated close ties with FDR. The latter seemed, at first, to be inclined to follow Stimson's advice and use a big stick against agressors. However, during his first term and most of his second, Roosevelt chose to avoid any major challenge to Japan or Hitler's Germany.

Apart from Stimson, few Americans cheered Roosevelt's 1937 speech threatening to "quarantine" Japan for her aggression in China. To

Stimson's disgust, Roosevelt seemed to bow to political pressure; he let more than a year pass before he again challenged Japanese expansionism. In early 1939, Japan announced her "new order" in East Asia, and coolly seized the island of Hainan. Roosevelt responded by ending the U.S.-Japan Commercial Treaty. This was followed by the Nazi-Soviet nonaggression pact, which left Russia free to attack Japan. Yet the double blow failed to deter Japan's military rulers.

The outbreak of general war in Europe, in September 1939, made it all but inevitable that America would join the Allied side. Roosevelt called for revision of the neutrality laws to allow the Allies to buy arms in America on a "cash and carry" basis, as was done in the years before World War I. Stimson fully concurred. He was one of the minority of public men at this time who urged the President to go still further. In an October 1939 radio speech, Stimson warned that a "time might well come when the only way to preserve the security of the people of the United States would be to fight for that security." Dean Acheson was among the first to join the campaign for intervention, as described in Chapter 4.

Would Hitler conquer all of Europe? How long would Britain and France be able to hold out? Would the American people support a policy of aiding them by "all means short of war"? These were among the major questions President Roosevelt faced between Hitler's invasion of Poland and the Japanese attack on Pearl Harbor.

Roosevelt decided that the times called for the first major test of the Stimson doctrine--the idea that America should seek to halt aggression through progressively tighter economic and military pressures. A new term,"nonbelligerent," was coined to describe America's status in this period. From 1939 onward, the line separating the United States from actual involvement in the European war became thinner and thinner. America was increasingly mobilized on a wartime basis, and its forces engaged in increasingly hostile acts against the main enemy, Germany. Although only economic pressures were used against Japan, these were viewed by the Japanese as a direct threat to their survival.

For all the differences between this new form of "nonbelligerency" and our neutrality in 1914-17, there was one important similarity. In both cases, the President of the United States chose to wait for an overt attack from the other side before seeking a declaration of war. Like Wilson, Roosevelt allowed the enemy to time his first major blow, which he knew would unite the American people.

In the spring of 1940, Hitler's armies gained a series of lightning victories in Denmark, Norway, Belgium, Holland, and Luxembourg. These drew from Roosevelt a promise, hardly neutral in tone:

> In our American unity, we will pursue two obvious and simultaneous courses: we will extend to the opponents of force the material resources of this nation, and at the same time we will harness and speed up the use of those resources in order that we ourselves in the Americas may have equipment and training equal to the task of any emergency and every defense.

On June 18, four days before France surrendered, Stimson delivered a radio speech that called for even more drastic measures. He told his listeners that the United States "today faces probably the greatest crisis in its history." He listed measures he considered necessary: repeal of the Neutrality Act, opening U.S. ports to the British and French navies and merchant marine, increasing production of arms for the

Allies, using American ships and convoys to deliver them, and adopting a system of universal military training.[2]

Two days later, on June 20, 1940, Roosevelt telephoned Stimson and asked him to join his cabinet as Secretary of War. Stimson who was nearly seventy-three, knew that FDR had been considering him for the job, yet he was astonished and delighted by the offer when it came. Roosevelt told his friend that everybody was "running around at loose ends in Washington." He said Stimson would be a stablizing factor in whom both the Army and the public would have confidence.

Stimson was as vulnerable as most people to Roosevelt's charm; he took the job not knowing whether he would be kept on after the November election. It was no secret that his appointment was intended to blunt Republican criticism of Roosevelt's decision to seek a third term.

Stimson's confirmation hearings before the Senate Committee on Military Affairs dramatized the growing assertiveness of the executive branch in the face of a global crisis. Several leading Republican Senators, notably Robert A. Taft, attacked Stimson for joining a Democratic administration. A number of Congressmen also considered him a war-monger. Stimson took the position that, if confirmed, his duties would not overlap with those of the Secretary of State. "Policy is determined by other branches of the Government," he noted dryly, "and it is [the Secretary of War's] duty to prepare for the troubles that may be brought about by their determinations."

Senator Arthur Vandenberg, a leading Republican specialist on foreign affairs, got high marks in Stimson's diary for his questions. They centered on whether the actions recommended in Stimson's radio speech would lead to war.

Stimson argued that they were legitimate acts of self-defense and that America was involved in an emergency in which traditional rules of conduct no longer applied.

Senator Taft asked the most unfriendly questions. Would Stimson favor giving credits to the British if they ran out of money? Would he go to war to prevent the defeat of England? Stimson replied carefully that the question of credits to the British would depend on the circumstances at the time, and so, even more, would the question of war. In exasperation, he told Taft "you have got to refrain from asking dogmatic questions and I have to refrain from answering such questions."

In his diary, Stimson lamented the fact that the son of President Taft, his old chief, "should try to gain his end by a cross-examination so narrow and mistrusting." Yet Stimson more than held his own, and his nomination was easily approved. Over the months ahead, he would find that Congress contained "some of the ablest and most farsighted men in the country,"

> and with their help the essential measures were passed, but the hearings and debates also became a sounding board for the hopelessly twisted views of a small group of men who, in the name of peace, would have kept America from acting to delay or block the greatest aggression in history.[3]

Stimson's first, and in some ways his most remarkable achievement while serving in FDR's cabinet was to persuade Congress to pass the nation's first peacetime draft law in the midst of a hard-fought presidential election, in which Roosevelt made his famous promise:

> We will not participate in foreign wars, and we will not send our army,

forces to fight in foreign lands outside the Americas, except in case of attack.

The enactment of the draft law greatly increased the power of the executive branch. Roosevelt had been unwilling to champion the draft in an election year. As a result, General George Marshall, the Chief of Staff of the Army, had only sponsored a strong program for voluntary enlistments. Stimson apparently persuaded both Roosevelt and Marshall to endorse a conscription bill in Congress. Marshall testified in its support, and it finally passed in September 1940. (This foreshadowed Marshall's role, a decade later, in presenting Truman's conscription bill to Congress after the outbreak of the Korean War.)

An even tougher legislative battle to extend the tour of draftees was waged a year later by Stimson, with Marshall again playing a key role. They won that fight in Congress by exactly one vote. Stimson had devoted nearly a lifetime to lobbying for peacetime conscription. It can be said that few institutions did more to reinforce a sense of common national purpose in the 1940s and 1950s--and few did more to deepen the divisions of American society after we became involved in Indochina for objectives no president could adequately explain.

The Road to Pearl Harbor

Meanwhile, Stimson also had the satisfaction of seeing the United States apply sanctions against Japan, as he had long proposed. The collapse of France in June 1940 was followed shortly by a Japanese ultimatum to the French Governor-General in Indochina. Roosevelt approved an embargo on sales of high grade scrap metals and aviation fuel to Japan. In September 1940, Japan signed the Tripartite Pact with Germany and Italy; the Vichy French then made a deal to remain in control of Indochina but to place the territory entirely at the disposal of Japan's war machine. Seeing no further reason to temporize, Roosevelt extended his embargo to apply to all scrap metals and oil.

The tempo of U.S. support for Britain increased rapidly after Roosevelt's reelection in November. The Land-Lease Act, which Congress passed in March 1941, allowed the President to transfer any article, service, or piece of information he chose to the government of any country he considered "vital" to the defense of the United States. This virtually eliminated the problem of Allied war debts, which had created so much trouble after the 1914-18 war.

Stimson, of course, sided with those in the administration who favored Lend-Lease. He denied that it was in violation of U.S. statutes and international law. He also argued that there was no need to go to Congress for authority. The exchange of destroyers for bases, Stimson asserted, was simply an exercise of the "traditional power of the Executive in foriegn affairs."[4]

Roosevelt was astute enough to know that few Americans would see things in that light. In early 1941, he submitted the Lend-Lease Act of Congress. Stimson testified on its behalf, repeating his familiar view that the Kellogg-Briand pact had changed international law and made it possible for a "nonbelligerent" to prohibit trade by its nationals with an "aggressor" nation. Stimson was asked at the Lend-Lease hearings if he would send supplies to Britain-- and if this would lead to war. "As Secretary of War," he replied cautiously,

> I became subordinate to the President and was directed to follow out his policies, and those policies, as I understand them, have always been, as shown by many, many occasions, a

desire, if possible--to effect the safety of this country without becoming involved in any warlike or forcible or military measures.

Roosevelt's artful maneuvering to keep public opinion on his side was sometimes intensely irritating to Stimson, though he never let this be known publicly. He had developed a close working relationship with Secretary of State Hull, and he accepted the need for Hull's talks with the Japanese Ambassador as a stalling device while U.S. forces were preparing for battle.

When Japan moved into southern Indochina in July 1951, Roosevelt responded by freezing Japanese assets in the United States. Britain and the Netherlands quickly followed suit. Japan was thereby denied sources of vital raw materials in the United States and Southeast Asia. Its navy would not have enough oil to complete the conquest of the "Greater East Asian Co-Prosperity Sphere" unless that task were begun before the winter monsoon season. Thus, in early September, the Japanese government decided to launch a full-scale invasion of Southeast Asia.

However, Japanese leaders decided to make one final effort to negotiate an agreement with the United States that would leave them free to pursue their goals. If no agreement were reached by early October, war must follow. The deadline was later extended a few weeks because the Imperial court, the navy, and elements of the army were reluctant to embark on a course that could mean disaster.

The Roosevelt administration knew about these developments in Japanese policy as they occurred, thanks to the so-called MAGIC intercepts of Tokyo's messages to its embassies abroad. However, they failed to spot the clues in intercepted messages that might have told them that Pearl Harbor would be attacked.

Meanwhile, Roosevelt and Churchill held their first summit conference at Argentia, Newfoundland, in August 1941. They announced that their common purpose was "the final destruction of Nazi tyranny." For all practical purposes, America and Britain were allied against Germany, though not against Japan. Since Hitler's attack on the Soviet Union, which relieved some of the pressure on Britain, American statemen had been arranging with Stalin for the extension of Lend-Lease aid to Russia.

As the de facto head of a grand alliance against Hitler, Roosevelt's options were now very limited. He must avoid being drawn prematurely into a war with Japan which might divert needed resources from the task of defeating Hitler. Yet he must also give no sign that he would ignore the threat Japan posed to China or to British or Dutch possessions in Asia, because this could demoralize our Allies at a critical stage of the war. Stimson's diary entries for this period show that he was well aware of these constraints.

Meanwhile, Lend-Lease aid to Russia meant convoying merchant ships all the way to Murmansk. To permit the British Royal Navy to assume this added burden, the U.S. Navy began escorting British merchant ships from the United States to Iceland in July 1941.

Several months earlier, on Stimson's advice, Roosevelt had assigned the U.S. Navy to submarine patrol duty in the North Atlantic from the U.S. coast out to 26 degrees west longitude. Until September 1941, U.S. vessels only signaled the position of German submarines to the Royal Navy. But when a German u-boat fired its torpedoes at an American destroyer on September 4 (missing its target), Roosevelt ordered U.S. ships to shoot on sight whenever they found a German submarine.

On November 17, after the Germans sank two American destroyers with a loss of 107 crewmen, Congress passed a bill that eliminated virtually all restrictions on arming merchant ships. The vote suggested that a declaration of war might also pass Congress by a narrow margin. Stimson and some of his colleagues felt that it was already long overdue, but Roosevelt still held back. As late as November 5, 1941, a national poll showed the American people opposing a declaration of war against Germany by a margin of 63 to 26 percent. Roosevelt still hoped to maneuver Hitler into striking first.

When the blow came, it was struck by the wrong enemy and in the wrong place. There is no evidence that the Roosevelt administration sought to provoke a Japanese attack on Pearl Harbor with the consequent heavy loss of men and ships. However, the administration was plainly negligent in not giving this possibility enough attention. Earlier intelligence reports had told them of Japanese interest in U.S. air and naval bases there.

Stimson and others knew that the whole scenario had been enacted in 1932 during a major series of U.S. war games and maneuvers in the Hawaiian Islands. Yet when intercepted messages told him that a major Japanese attack was near, he assumed that it would be aimed somewhere in Southeast Asia. Later, he did everything in his power to ensure that all of the blame for the Pearl Harbor disaster fell on the local Army commander and not on himself.[5]

Wartime Decisions

Right after Pearl Harbor, thousands of Americans of Japanese descent were rounded up and placed in concentration camps on the entirely unsubstantiated grounds that they were endangering U.S. national security. Stimson has been singled out by some historians to answer for this injustice, since it was carried out under the rubric of "military necessity." It is true that he approved the policy on these grounds and contributed to a massive violation of civil rights. However, President Roosevelt himself must bear the ultimate responsibility for this entirely political decision. It remains one of the most disturbing reminders in our history that expanding the powers of the presidency can directly diminish the freedom of individual U.S. citizens.

After Pearl Harbor, Stimson's main responsibility was to assure that U.S. forces had the arms and supplies they needed at the right time and place. Under his aegis, extraordinary logistical and administrative feats were performed, not least of which was the top-secret Manhattan Project, the building of the atomic bomb.

At one point, Stimson became so obsessed with his role as expeditor of war production that he even suggested legislation to allow the President to draft civilians for work in war plants. Fortunately for his own reputation--and for the U.S. war effort, which would surely have been harmed by such a law--no labor draft was ever enacted. Nevertheless, the incident illustrates the almost limitless power Stimson was prepared to confer upon the President.

FDR did not, on the whole, seek the advice of his Secretary of War on matters of grand strategy. For this, he relied mainly on the Combined Staff (British and American) over which General Marshall presided. Stimson himself rarely took a position that was in conflict with Marshall's, and he never did so publicly. However, Stimson did play an important role in trying to persuade Churchill to agree to give priority to a cross-channel invasion of France instead of operations aimed at the "soft underbelly" of Europe.

The Postwar Period

In matters relating to the postwar status of conquered and occupied territories, Stimson's views were not unlike Churchill's. He helped dissuade Roosevelt from adopting Treasury Secretary Morgenthau's plan to limit Germany's postwar economy to subsistence farming. (This revealed Morgenthau's ignorance of the political and economic consequences of milder economic measures imposed on Germany after World War I.)

In regard to Japan, Stimson was instrumental in the important U.S. decision to preserve the institution of the Emperor. However, he did recommend to Truman that atomic bombs be dropped on Hiroshima and Nagasaki (while sparing the old capital of Kyoto). From Stimson's writings, it is quite evident that he meant the atomic bombs to impress Stalin, whose uncooperative attitude was already a source of grave concern in Washington.

Yet it was Stimson who argued, during his final months of service to President Truman, against the tendency among some of his colleagues to overreact to Soviet behavior in Eastern Europe. Stimson held that the U.S. government should continue to regard the Balkan states as "beyond the proper sphere of United States action."[6] As we shall see, this advice was not very different from that offered by George Kennan, whose concept of "containment" ruled out the notion of "liberating" Eastern Europe.

FOOTNOTES

[1] Henry L. Stimson was born in 1868 (six years before Churchill). The Stimsons were an old and prominent New York family, whose members had served in nearly every American war. Stimson's father earned a fortune early in life as a banker, then devoted the remainder of his career to the study and practice of medicine.

[2] Congress complied with Roosevelt's request for defense spending authority that shattered all peacetime records: $5 billion for the year beginning July 1, 1940 and $11 billion more in future contracts.

[3] Henry L. Stimson and McGeorge Bundy, On Active Service in Peace and War, New York: Harper and Row, 1948, p. 330.

[4] Richard Current, Secretary Stimson, New Brunswick, N.J.: Rutgers University Press, 1965, pp. 148-49. Stimson dug out an 1892 Statute that allowed the Secretary of War to lease Army property; he argued that this would permit FDR to trade the destroyers to Britain without going to Congress for a new law. This high-handed approach foreshadowed later clashes between the executive branch and Congress.

[5] See Richard N. Current, op.cit., pp. 164-88. The atmosphere in Washington had changed markedly since a decade earlier when Stimson refused to look at an intercepted message on the grounds that "gentlemen do not read each other's mail."

[6] Henry L. Stimson and McGeorge Bundy, On Active Service in Peace and War, pp. 634-655. He later reversed his position and supported aid to Greece and Turkey.

George F. Kennan

Chapter 3

GEORGE KENNAN: AUTHOR AND CRITIC

OF THE CONTAINMENT POLICY

At the close of World War II, George Kennan was the second-ranking American diplomat in Moscow. Few people outside the State Department had heard of him, but he was destined to play a key role in shaping our postwar policy of "containment." Later, in 1950, he would leave the Department and begin a new role as historian and critic of U.S. foreign policy. He argued against what he saw as Washington's overreliance on military means to halt communist expansion. To Kennan, military force was important, but it was only one dimension of the problem.

A career diplomat and Soviet specialist, Kennan had more first-hand knowledge and insight into the workings of the Soviet government than any other American of his generation.[1] To him, it seemed plain that Franklin Roosevelt's concept of "Four Policemen"--Russia, Britain, China, and the United States--running the postwar world was dangerously naive. Kennan had watched and reported on Stalin's massive purge in the 1930s, his non-aggression pact with Hitler in 1939, and the subsequent deportation to central Russia of hundreds of thousands of people from the Baltic states.

When Hitler attacked his erstwhile Russian ally in June 1941, Kennan was in charge of the U.S. Embassy in Berlin. He recognized that we must join with the Soviets and the British to defeat Hitler's aggression, but he hoped the United States would not aid or support Stalin's goal of controlling Eastern Europe.

Six months later, the United States was finally at war against the Axis powers. Kennan and the American Embassy staff were first interned for several months and then exchanged in Portugal. Kennan's wartime assignments included service on the European Advisory Commission, which tried to sort out the growing conflicts between Soviet, British and American policies toward conquered and occupied territories.

Kennan's worst fears about Soviet aims in Eastern Europe were abundantly confirmed by events such as the Katyn Forest massacre of thousands of Polish officer prisoners. Meanwhile in Washington, President Roosevelt took a very different view of U.S.-Soviet relations. He was confidant he could persuade Stalin to rise above his petty suspicions and territorial aims and play the role of a true world statesman after the war. Moreover, Roosevelt believed he owed Stalin something to compensate for the delay in opening a Western front.[2] For the sake of harmony, Roosevelt was prepared not to contest Stalin's claims in Eastern Europe too vigorously, provided nothing was done that would arouse the anger of the millions of Americans whose families originated in that part of Europe.

Just after the Normandy landings, Stalin began to move more boldly to consolidate his hold on neighboring states. In August, Radio Moscow incited the non-communist Polish underground to rise up against the Nazis in Warsaw. For two months, the Poles fought a losing fight against the well-armed German garrison, while Red Army tank units waited nearby on the banks of the Vistula; Stalin refused to help the Western Allies resupply the Poles from the air. For people in the Western world, news of his maneuver was partly muted by the liberation of France.

During the summer of 1944, Kennan traveled to Moscow via Iran to take up his duties as Minister-Counselor of the American Embassy. When

Ambassador Averell Harriman first offered him the assignment, Kennan told him that his views on postwar cooperation with Russia were far less optimistic than Roosevelt's. Harriman accepted him for the post anyway.

In September 1944, Kennan reported that Soviet officials who opposed cooperation with the United States seemed to be winning out over those who favored good relations; "the policy appears to be crystallizing to force us and the British to accept all Soviet policies backed by strength and the prestige of the Red Army." Kennan submitted a 35-page dispatch developing this theme, but official Washington was not receptive to these views at the time.

In February 1945, Roosevelt, Churchill and Stalin had their first summit at Yalta. Roosevelt's health was failing rapidly, and he was unable to focus effectively on many of the issues. Questions of enormous importance, such as the political future of Germany, were dealt with in a matter of hours or even minutes.

Throughout most of the war, Roosevelt, Churchill and Stalin had maintained their working relationship by concentrating on short-term military requirements. With Hitler's defeat near, political issues such as the future of Poland began to crowd the agenda. It is hardly surprising that many of the "agreements" reached at Yalta were highly superficial and incomplete. They provided a fruitful source of later disagreement between the Soviet and U.S. governments--and between Roosevelt's successor and the U.S. Congress.

Throughout Roosevelt's final month, Kennan watched these events with worried eyes. He saw that the President tended to yield on secondary matters whenever the Russians produced a display of bad temper or rudeness--hoping to earn Stalin's gratitude and cooperation on primary issues. These tactics, which often worked with an ally who shared his values, did not succeed with Stalin.

In Moscow, Harriman, Kennan and General John Dean, chief of the U.S. military mission, all believed that President Roosevelt was right in wanting to maintain close ties with Stalin after the war. They believed that East-West cooperation was both desirable and attainable. However, they felt that Washington officials tended to overrate the importance of Soviet cooperation to the achievement of America's postwar aims. The United States would emerge from the war incomparably stronger than Russia, both militarily and economically. Its sociopolitical system based on individual freedom had survived for over a hundred and fifty years, while the Soviet police state was relatively new and untried.

To improve relations with Russia, the Americans in Moscow favored the exact reverse of Roosevelt's tactics.[3] U.S. negotiators should avoid placing themselves in the position of supplicants by constantly stressing America's dependence on Soviet cooperation to achieve our postwar objectives. They should refuse to let themselves be browbeaten by calculated Russian displays of anger and rudeness. They must match their Soviet counterparts in stubborn patience, making certain that each aspect of any agreement was clearly understood and based on mutual advantage. Then, but only then, according to these experienced diplomats, would Soviet leaders abide by their agreements.

In the last weeks of Roosevelt's life and the first weeks of Harry Truman's administration, Americans in Moscow began to fear that Washington might suddenly swing to the other extreme in its dealings with the Soviet Union. Having tried to charm the Russians into cooperating with America's plans for the postwar world--and having gained little in return except abuse--some U.S.

officials were beginning to look upon Russia as a virtual enemy and a serious threat to American security interests.

Stalin was obviously shaken by Roosevelt's death on April 12; he expressed his concern to Ambassador Harriman about the continuity of American policy. Harriman assured him that U.S. policy remained the same and used the occasion to ask Stalin to reverse an earlier decision and send Foreign Minister Molotov to San Francisco to take part in the founding of the United Nations. Stalin agreed, and Molotov stopped off in Washington on the same day that Moscow published its mutual aid treaty with Warsaw. This treaty caused a furor in Washington and resulted in a tense meeting between Molotov and President Truman.

Molotov said the only obstacle to a settlement in Poland was Western opposition to the new Soviet formula of twenty-one communists and six non-communists in the Warsaw government. Truman told the Foreign Minister bluntly that Stalin had made an agreement on Poland and all that was needed was for his government to keep its word. He said he wanted friendship with Russia but this could not be a "one-way street." When Molotov said he had never been spoken to that way in his life, Truman advised him to keep his agreements and he would not be spoken to that way.

Some historians have argued that this incident reveals a sudden hardening of U.S. policy after Roosevelt's death. However, Truman's harshness may have been exaggerated by his biographers. He did his best to salvage the wartime policy of collaboration with Russia.

Truman and the man he chose to be his first Secretary of State, James Byrnes, shared the country's bouyant optimism at the end of World War II. During the remainder of 1945 and 1946,

Secretary Byrnes was often out of the country attending meetings of the Big Four foreign ministers. These long weeks of negotiation finally produced peace treaties for the former Axis satellites: Bulgaria, Finland, Hungary, Italy, and Rumania. However, except for the treaty with Italy, these merely confirmed the terms Russia had dictated to its smaller neighbors in wartime armistice agreements. George Kennan described Byrnes's negotiating technique at the December 1945 foreign ministers meeting in Moscow:

> He plays his negotiations by ear, going into them with no clear or fixed plan, with no definite set objectives or limitations. He relies entirely on his own agility and presence of mind and hopes to take advantage of tactical openings. In the present conference his weakness in dealing with the Russians is that his main purpose is to achieve some sort of an agreement, he doesn't much care what. The realities behind this agreement, since they concern only such people as Koreans, Rumanians, and Iranians, about whom he knows nothing, do not concern him. He wants an agreement for its political effect at home. The Russians know this. They will see that for this superficial success he pays a heavy price in the things that are real.[4]

Prominent Republicans in the U.S. delegation such as John Foster Dulles were more aware than Byrnes of the American public's growing irritation with Russia. At each succeeding conference, they became more critical of the Secretary of State. By mid-1946, Truman had decided to replace Byrnes with General George C. Marshall, although the change did not take place until the following year.

As Kennan saw it, the problems of U.S. policy toward Russia and Germany were often linked. Of the many issues that divided the American and Soviet governments in this period, the question of how to deal with Germany was the most critical. The occupying powers faced an enormous task in simply keeping the destitute and demoralized German people alive. The problem was aggravated by the fact that the Soviet Union, in redrawing the map of Poland, had forced 9 million Germans out of areas east of the Oder-Neisse line. These people, along with 2.5 million Germans expelled from Czechoslovakia and half a million more from Hungary, had to make a new life for themselves within Germany's reduced boundaries.

Instead of cooperating with international relief efforts, Soviet officials concentrated on extracting whatever they could in the way of reparations from their zone of Germany; they also refused to meet their commitments to send surplus food to the Western allies' zones. The Four-Power Control Council, which could only operate on the basis of unanimity, was often dead-locked by Soviet dissent. The same pattern of U.S.-Soviet relations had begun to emerge worldwide. The reactions of Americans ranged from bewilderment to bitter denunciations.

Kennan's "Long Telegram"

On February 22, 1946, George Kennan was in charge of the American Embassy in Moscow. He was also suffering, his Memoirs tell us, from a cold, fever, sinusitis, toothache, and the aftereffects of a sulfa drug. Among the papers brought to his sickroom that morning was a message from the U.S. Treasury Department asking why the Russians were unwilling to join the new World Bank and Monetary Fund. Kennan's scorn for this naive query gave him strength to respond with an eight thousand word telegraphic essay;

he described Soviet policy as expansionist and unable to conceive of permanent coexistence with the United States. Coping with this force, he said, "is undoubtedly [the] greatest task our diplomacy has ever faced."

Kennan did not offer a detailed plan in his "long telegram," as it came to be known. However, he stated his belief that "the problem is within our power to solve," because the Soviet Union was "highly sensitive to the logic of force. . . . Thus, if the adversary has sufficient force and makes clear his readiness to use it, he rarely has to do so." Much would depend on the "cohesion, firmness, and vigor which [the] Western world can muster" and on "the health and vigor of our own society."[5] As conceived by Kennan, "containment" bore no resemblance to a policy of military encirclement of the Soviet Union.

Kennan's "long telegram" reached Washington just when top officials were in a mood to pay attention to it. Two weeks earlier, Stalin had delivered a speech restating the Marxist-Leninist dogma of "inevitable war" between communism and capitalism; he proposed a series of Five-Year plans to prepare the Soviet Union for this struggle. Two weeks after Kennan's long telegram arrived, Churchill delivered his "iron curtain" speech at Fulton, Missouri, calling for a "fraternal association of the English-speaking peoples" to defend the Western world.

Containment in Practice

Gradually, the Truman administration adopted (and then began to modify) Kennan's concept of containment. Soviet pressures in Iran and Turkey and their continuing refusal to cooperate in Germany helped to crystallize the U.S. position.

In Iran, Soviet and British forces had each occupied portions of the country during the war to forestall growing German influence. After the British withdrew, the Soviets appeared to consolidate their influence in the country. However, faced with Anglo-American warnings, Soviet forces were pulled out in March 1946. In the case of Turkey, the Soviets steadily increased their demands for political and military rights which would have reduced the country to a Soviet protectorate. In August 1946, the United States responded by sending a naval task force into the eastern Mediterranean.

Each of these moves appeared to reduce temporarily the Soviet pressures, or at least to redirect them to other areas. They neither led to war nor produced any permanent relaxation of tensions; Soviet advances always seemed to follow the course of least resistance. As Dean Acheson later recalled, "The year 1946 was for the most part a year of learning that minds in the Kremlin worked very much as George F. Kennan had predicted they would."

Kennan's reputation and influence mushroomed overnight. He was reassigned to Washington to develop a course for senior officials at the National War College. Then, in 1947, when General Marshall took charge of the State Department, Kennan became Director of the new Policy Planning Staff. He had Secretary Marshall's full support, and he made major contributions to the basic strategy of the Marshall Plan. For example, he correctly predicted that, if the Soviets were offered a chance to take part in the program, they would decline--and thus assume the onus for dividing Europe.

New Approach to Japan

Kennan also helped reshape U.S. policy toward Japan in this period. In 1948, he was sent on a mission to Japan to reevaluate the basic principles of the U.S. occupation. Many of the original occupation goals had been achieved or now seemed excessively meddlesome and out of date. Once Kennan managed to gain access to General MacArthur, he found they could agree on most issues. The problem was MacArthur's hugh occupation staff, which had developed a vested interest in carrying on the original policies. These included dismantling Japan's industrial combines and purging hundreds of thousands of Japanese from the government.

Kennan's mission helped produce the necessary momentum for a basic change of emphasis in U.S. policy toward Japan. The purge was ended. Greater attention was given to economic recovery. Plans were also laid for a peace treaty and to permit Japan to rearm for self-defense, though these steps were not altogether in accord with Kennan's recommendations.

In fact, Kennan had grave doubts about the administration's policy as it began to emerge in 1950. He favored a U.S.-Soviet agreement by which both powers would recognize Japan's neutrality. Although he wanted Japan to be equipped with adequate internal and coastal defense forces, he objected to the de facto alignment of Japan with a vast new anti-communist Asian alliance. As we have seen, he objected even more basically to the perversion (as he saw it) of his containment policy into a rationale for ringing the Soviet Union and China with American "forward" bases.

The seeds of this new approach were planted earlier by a man whom Kennan greatly admired.

Secretary Marshall had assumed President Truman would lose the 1948 election. Thus, he did little to prepare the American public for Chiang Kai-shek's impending defeat in China. The blame for "losing China" fell on Dean Acheson, Marshall's successor. Under heavy pressure from right-wing forces in Congress, the Truman administration began in early 1950 to reorient its policy--from the use of economic aid to contain Soviet influence in Europe to military containment of Chinese communism in Asia.

Kennan remained an influential figure in the State Department until the outbreak of the Korean War in 1950. However, he was not invited to take part in the key discussions which shaped America's response to the North Korean attack. Kennan was critical of the administration's decisions--to cross the 38th parallel into North Korea and to use the war as a pretext to isolate China politically and economically from the rest of the world.

For these and other reasons, Kennan retired from the Foreign Service in 1950, and began a highly fruitful second career as an historian at the Institute for Advanced Study in Princeton. He resumed his diplomatic career on three occasions: to help negotiate the end of the Korean War with Soviet Ambassador Malik at the United Nations, to serve as Ambassador to the Soviet Union from 1951 to 1953, and finally to serve as President Kennedy's Ambassador to Yugoslavia.

During the 1970's, Kennan often defended the concept of detente with the USSR against conservative critics, though he pointed out that Nixon and Kissinger oversold the idea of detente to the American people, thereby inviting overreaction as soon as some of their policies began to go sour.

Kennan was even more critical of the Carter administration's response to the Soviet invasion of Afghanistan. On February 1, 1980, he published an article in the New York Times that has all the intellectual vigor and stylistic strength of his earlier work. We reproduce the article in full, because it represents perhaps a unique commentary on U.S.-Soviet relations in the 1980's by one of the greatest figures of the post-World War II era of American foreign policy:

Princeton, N.J. On Christmas Day 1979, after more than a century of periodic involvement with the internal affairs of its turbulent neighbor, and after many months of futile effort to find a pro-Soviet Afghan figure capable of running the country, the Soviet Government suddenly expanded what was already a sizeable military involvement in Afghanistan into a full-fledged occupation, promising that the troops would leave when their limited mission had been accomplished.

This move was not only abrupt--no effort had been made to prepare world opinion for it--but it was executed with incredible political clumsiness. The pretext offered was an insult to the intelligence of even the most credulous of Moscow's followers. The world community was left with no alternative but to condemn the operation in the strongest terms, and it has done so.

So bizarre was the Soviet action that one is moved to wonder whence exactly, in the closely shielded recesses of Soviet policy making, came the inspiration for it and the political influence to achieve its approval. It was a move decidedly not in character

for either Aleksei N. Kosygin or
Leonid I. Brezhnev. (The one was,
of course, ill and removed from
active work. The limitations on the
other's health and powers of attention
are well-known.) Andrei A. Gromyko,
too, is unlikely to have approved it.
These reflections suggest the recent
breakthrough, to positions of dominant
influence, of hard-line elements much
less concerned for world opinion,
but also much less experienced, than
those older figures.

Such a change was not unexpected
by the more attentive Kremlinologists,
particularly in the light of the recent
deterioration of Soviet-American
relations, but it was assumed that it
would take place only in connection
with, and coincidental with, the
retirement of Mr. Brezhnev and other
older Politburo members. That it
could occur with the preservation of
Mr. Brezhnev as a figurehead was not
foreseen.

Be that as it may, this ill-consi-
dered move was bound to be unacceptable
to the world community, and the United
States had no alternative but to join
in the condemnation of it in the United
Nations. But beyond that point, the
American official reaction has revealed
a disquieting lack of balance, both in
the analysis of the problem and then,
not surprisingly, in the response to it.

In the official American interpre-
tation of what occurred in Afghanistan,
no serious account appears to have been
taken of such specific factors as
geographic proximity, ethnic affinity of
peoples on both sides of the border, and

political instability in what is after all, a border country of the Soviet Union. Now, specific factors of this nature, all suggesting defensive rather than offensive impulses, may not have been all there was to Soviet motivation, nor would they have sufficed to justify the action; but they were relevant to it and should have been given their due in any realistic appraisal of it.

Instead of this, the American view of the Soviet action appears to have run overwhelmingly to the assumption that it was a prelude to aggressive military moves against various countries and regions farther afield. No one can guarantee, of course, that one or another such move will not take place.

A war atmosphere has been created. Discussion in Washington has been dominated by talk of American military responses--of the acquisition of bases and facilities, of the creation of a rapid-deployment force, of the cultivation of military ties with other countries all along Russia's sensitive southern border. In these circumstances, anything can happen. But the fact is, this extravagant view of Soviet motivation rests, to date, exclusively on our own assumptions. I am not aware of any substantiation of it in anything the Soviet leaders themselves have said or done. On the contrary, Mr. Brezhnev has specifically, publically and vigorously denied any such intentions.

In the light of these assumptions we have been prodigal with strident public warnings to the Russians, some of them issued even prior to the occupation of Afghanistan, not to attack this place or that, assuring them that if they did so, we would respond by military means. Can this really be sound procedure? Warnings of this nature are implicit accusations as well as commitments. We are speaking here of a neighboring area of the Soviet Union, not of the United States. Aside from the question of whether we could really back up these pronouncements if our hand were to be called, is it really wise--is it not in fact a practice pregnant with responsibilities for resentment and misreading of signals--to go warning people publicly not to do things they have never evinced any intention of doing?

This distortion in our assessment of the Soviet motivation has affected, not unnaturally, our view of other factors in the Middle Eastern situation. What else but a serious lack of balance could explain our readiness to forget, in the case of Pakistan, the insecurity of the present Government, its recent callous jeopardizing of the lives of our embassy personnel, its lack of candor about its nuclear programs--and then to invite humiliation by pressing upon it offers of military aid that elicited only insult and contempt? What else could explain, in the case of Iran, our sudden readiness--if only the hostages were released--to forget not only their sufferings but all the flag-burnings, the threatening fists, the hate-ridden faces and the cries of "death to Carter," and to offer to take these very people to our bosoms in a common resistance to Soviet aggressiveness? What else could explain our naive hope that the Arab states could be induced, just by the shock of Afghanistan, to forget their differences with Israel and to join us in an effort to contain the supposedly power-mad Russians?

This last merits a special word. I have already referred to the war atmosphere in Washington. Never since World War II has there been so far-reaching a militarization of thought and discourse in the capital. An unsuspecting stranger, plunged into its midst, could only conclude that the last hope of peaceful, nonmilitary solutions had been exhausted--that from now on only weapons, however used, could count.

These words are not meant to express opposition to a prompt and effective strengthening of our military capabilities relevant to the Middle East. If what was involved here was the carrying of a big stick while speaking softly rather than the carrying of a relatively small stick while thundering all over the place, who could object? But do we not, by this preoccupation with a Soviet military threat the reality of which remains to be proved run the risk of forgetting that the greatest real threats to our security in that region remain what they have been all along: our self-created dependence on Arab oil and our involvement in a wholly unstable Israeli-Arab relationship, neither of which is susceptible of correction by purely military means, and in neither of which is the Soviet Union and major factor?

If the Persian Gulf is really vital to our security, it is surely we who, by our unrestrained greed for oil, have made it so. Would it not be better to set about to eliminate, by a really serious and determined effort, a dependence that ought never have been allowed to arise, than to try to shore up by military means, in a highly unfavorable region, the unsound position into which the dependence has led us? Military force might conceivably become necessary as a supplement to such an effort; it could never be an adequate substitute for it.

The oddest expression of this lack of balance it perhaps in the bilateral measures with which we conceive ourselves to have punished the Russian actions. Aside from the fact that it is an open question whom we punished most by these measures--Russia or ourselves--we have portrayed them as illustrations of what could happen to Moscow if it proceeded to one or another of the further aggressive acts we credit it with plotting. But that is precisely what these measures are not; for they represent cards that have already been played and cannot be played twice. There was never any reason to suppose that the Soviet Government, its prestige once engaged, could be brought by open pressure of this nature to withdraw its troops from Afghanistan. But this means, then, that we have expended--for what was really a hopeless purpose--all the important nonmilitary cards we conceived ourselves as holding in our hand. Barring a resort to war, the Soviet Government has already absorbed the worst of what we have to offer, and has nothing further to fear from us. Was this really mature statesmanship on our part?

We are now in the danger zone. I can think of no instance in modern history where such a breakdown of political communication and such a triumph of unrestrained military suspicion as now marks Soviet-American relations has not led, in the end, to armed conflict. The danger is heightened by the fact that we do not know, at this time, with whom we really have to deal at the Soviet end. If there was ever a time for realism, prudence and restraint in American statesmanship, it is this one. Nothing in the passions of electoral politics could serve as the slightest excuse for ignoring this necessity.

FOOTNOTES

[1] Born in Wisconsin in 1904, Kennan identified closely with his uncle and namesake, an engineer who explored Siberia in the nineteenth century. He joined the newly established career Foreign Service in 1926, was sent first to Hamburg, and then began a three-year training program in the Russian language while serving in various Baltic consulates. He helped reopen the U.S. Embassy in Moscow in 1933 and was in charge of the embassy in Berlin when World War II began.

[2] Stalin's moods fluctuated widely. For a time in 1943, he stopped answering messages from Roosevelt and Churchill because they delayed opening a Western front against Hitler. After the invasion of Italy, Stalin was all smiles and agreed to a summit meeting at Teheran. However, the Soviets bitterly contested the Western allies' refusal to allow them a role in the occupation of Italy. Stalin and Molotov cited this precedent whenever Churchill or Roosevelt sought to influence political developments in Eastern Europe.

[3] See George F. Kennan, Memoirs, 1925-1950 (Boston: Little, Brown, 1967), pp. 213-264.

[4] Kennan, Memoirs, 1925-1950, pp. 302-303.

[5] George Kennan, Memoirs, 1925-1950, pp. 573-598.

Dean Acheson

Chapter 4

DEAN ACHESON: THE SEARCH FOR WORLD ORDER

The decade of the 1940s demanded greatness of a country that had been reluctant to assume the responsibilities of a major power. Hitler's threat to Western values left America no choice but to enter the war--and there was little doubt that she would emerge as the world's preeminent military and economic force.

Among American statesmen of this period, Dean Acheson had the clearest vision of how to use the opportunity it offered. He played a central role in creating the first global system of economic order, yet he was forced later by domestic pressures to give more emphasis to military containment of communism. During the final years of his life, Acheson remained an advocate of strong executive power, though he sometimes challenged his successors when power seemed to become an end in itself.

Born in Connecticut in 1893, Acheson attended Yale and Harvard Law School. After brief service in World War I, he went to Washington in 1919 as a clerk to Justice Louis Brandeis. Private law practice followed, and in 1933, he was recruited by his old teacher, Justice Felix Frankfurter, for Roosevelt's New Deal administration. Though Acheson soon rose to become Acting Secretary of the Treasury, he left when President Roosevelt abandoned the gold standard, because he regarded this as an act of selfish economic nationalism.

International Economic Policy

By 1939, Acheson had resumed his ties with the Roosevelt administration, heading a board that reviewed the fairness of rules regulating private business. In a speech at Yale two months after war broke out in Europe, he echoed Henry Stimson's call for rapid military preparation by the United States. However, Acheson also looked ahead toward the postwar world and saw a need to avoid the major problems that followed World War I.

In this speech at Yale, Acheson proposed a series of economic policies which he would later play a key role in implementing. He forecast a need for large capital investment to rebuild the European economy. He called for new global institutions that could manage exchange rates between countries and support currencies that were in temporary danger of collapse. And he underscored the problem of "exclusive or preferential trade arrangements with other areas created by military or financial conquest, agreement, or political connection." Acheson gave his full support to Secretary Cordell Hull's Reciprocal Trade Agreement program.

In 1940, Acheson moved a step closer to joining the administration by helping to frame its legal case for the Lend-Lease Act. He was more sensitive than Stimson to the need to rally Congressional support for this innovation.

In February 1941, Acheson was sworn in as Assistant Secretary of State for Economic Affairs. In this role, he gave the State Department--which heretofore had often yielded to Treasury on foreign economic policy--a major voice in the struggle to deny Hitler access to the resources of European neutrals. During the war years, he also represented the United States in negotiations which led to the creation of the

World Bank, the International Monetary Fund, the Food and Agriculture Organization, and the United Nations Relief and Rehabilitation Administration (UNRRA).

In December 1944, Acheson became Assistant Secretary for Congressional Relations--"chief lobbyist for State." This was a perfect training ground for his later responsibilities as Secretary. Older politicians, such as Vice President Truman, taught him the art of sharing public credit for policy with Senators whose support was needed. After Truman succeeded Roosevelt, he promoted Acheson to Undersecretary of State. This marked the beginning of a highly successful relationship based on complete mutual trust.

After Japan's surrender, Acheson's immediate task was to bring some order to our widely scattered efforts to aid the destitute peoples of allied and former enemy nations. During 1946, he also began to formulate a policy of helping weak states resist communist takeover. In early 1946, emergency loans of $25 million each were extended to Greece and Turkey. Acheson also planned the administration's effort to mediate the Chinese civil war. General Marshall accepted the thankless job of mediator on condition that Acheson would back-stop his efforts in Washington.

The Truman Doctrine

In January 1947, General Marshall replaced James Byrnes as Secretary of State. In the military tradition, he made Undersecretary Acheson his chief of staff. Acheson ran the Department, and Marshall took command of Congressional relations. Morale in the Department soared to an all-time high in this period under the most effective leadership team it has ever seen.

During February, the situation in Greece began to deteriorate rapidly. State Department officials estimated that only a coalition government and substantial foreign aid could save the country from an early communist takeover. On Friday, February 21, when General Marshall was out of town, the British Embassy delivered copies of two very important messages to Acheson. One applied to Greece, the other to Turkey; Britain could no longer afford to carry the main burden of aiding either of these countries and would cease to do so in six weeks. The British government hoped that the United States could assume this responsibility. Britain estimated the initial foreign exchange needs of Greece at from $240 million to $280 million. Smaller but still substantial sums would be needed by Turkey, which had a stronger government.

Acheson knew that the United States was faced with an historic challenge. As he and a team of State Department officials worked through the weekend on staff papers to brief the Secretary and President, Acheson realized there could be only one decision. By the afternoon of Monday, February 24, General Marshall and President Truman shared his conviction that strengthening Greece and Turkey was vital to U.S. security, and that America was the only country which could perform this task. However, funds and authority would have to be obtained from Congress. Since Marshall would leave for a Foreign Ministers meeting in less than a week, he asked Acheson to continue to direct the preparation of administration policy.

On Wednesday, February 26, the leaders of Congress, which was controlled by the Republicans, met with Truman and Acheson in the President's office. Opposition was already brewing in both parties against continued U.S. relief efforts in Europe; the Republicans wanted to cut the budget wherever possible. Thus, the meeting in the oval office took place in an atmosphere of confrontation.

President Truman's opening remarks were unimpressive and were received in chilly silence by the Congressmen. Acheson whispered to him a request to speak. He knew the members of Congress had no conception of the crisis they were facing. It was his task to bring it home to them. He later recalled saying that, during the past eighteen months,

> . . .Soviet pressure on the Straits, on Iran, and on northern Greece had brought the Balkans to the point where a highly possible Soviet breakthrough might open three continents to Soviet penetration. Like apples in a barrel infected by one rotten one, the corruption of Greece would infect Iran and all to the east. . . . The Soviet Union was playing one of the greatest gambles in history at minimal cost. It did not need to win all the possibilities. Even one or two offered immense gains. We and we alone were in a position to break up the play.[1]

A long silence followed Acheson's statement. Then Senator Arthur Vandenberg, Chairman of the Foreign Relations Committee, said, "Mr. President, if you will say that to the Congress and the country, I will support you and I believe that most of its members will do the same."

General Marshall flew to Moscow a few days later, leaving Acheson in charge of efforts to draw up a plan and to gain Congressional support. He told Acheson to disregard the possible effects of these efforts on the Foreign Ministers meeting; this was now less important than saving the pivotal position occupied by Greece and Turkey.

There was considerable controversy over the drafting of President Truman's message to Congress. George Kennan approved the objective of trying to save Greece and Turkey, but he thought the wording of the text supplied by the State

Department committed the United States too broadly. On the other hand, Clark Clifford (a young counsel to the President) thought the text needed strengthening; Acheson persuaded him to withdraw his suggestions. On March 12, President Truman delivered his speech to a joint session of Congress. The crucial passage was;

> I believe that it must be the policy of the United States to support free peoples who are resisting attempted subjugation by armed minorities or by outside pressures.
>
> I believe that we must assist free peoples to work out their own destinies in their own way.
>
> I believe that our help should be primarily through economic and financial aid which is essential to economic stability and orderly political processes.

This concept became known as the Truman Doctrine. By later standards, the amounts requested were not vast. But the ideas expressed were to have the broadest possible implications for United States policy. The President asked Congress to provide $250 million in aid to Greece and $150 million for Turkey. He also sought authority to send American civilian and military personnel to both countries to assist in reconstruction and military training.

Although the President received a standing ovation from the Congress at the end of his speech, Acheson saw this as a "tribute to a brave man rather than unanimous acceptance of his policy." It took two months of very hard work to persuade Congress to reverse its initial stand against foreign aid and approve this new policy. In his testimony, Acheson tried to dispel any impression that the Truman Doctrine was a blank check to weak governments everywhere.

The Marshall Plan Takes Shape

During the months that Congress debated aid to Greece and Turkey, the administration was studying the problems of Europe as a whole. Conditions in many parts of Europe during this bitter cold winter were in some respects worse than during wartime. Food was extremely scarce because the cities had neither goods nor sound currency to exchange; farmers produced mainly for their own consumption. War-damaged factories and transportation systems remained unrepaired. Unemployment rose to record heights as industrial production almost ceased for lack of coal, raw materials, and spare parts. Those who were lucky enough to have homes had little or no fuel to heat them. Under these conditions, class conflict and political antagonism became vicious.

In addition to Marshall and Acheson, the other key figures in shaping the U.S. response to this situation were Assistant Secretary of State Will Clayton and George Kennan, head of the new Policy Planning Staff. Clayton, who headed Acheson's old Bureau of Economic Affairs, analyzed the problem and prodded the administration to take action. Kennan tried to forecast the Soviet reaction to a major European recovery program. (It was agreed to invite the Soviets to take part--and let them bear the onus for dividing Europe if they refused.) Acheson served as coordinator of the administration's plans and political strategy. Marshall, who returned from Moscow on April 28, brought impressions of the Russian leaders' current aims.

It was Marshall who first announced to the world the basic concept of the plan that eventually bore his name. In his brief speech at the Harvard Commencement of June 1947, he described the existing conditions in Europe; then he explained how the concept related to Soviet-American relations. He said that U.S. policy was directed "not against any country or doctrine, but against hunger, poverty, desperation, and chaos." Thus

> Any government that is willing to assist in the task of recovery will find full cooperation, I am sure, on the part of the United States Government. Any government which maneuvers to block the recovery of other countries cannot expect help from us. Furthermore, governments, political parties, or groups which seek to perpetuate human misery in order to profit therefrom politically or otherwise will encounter the opposition of the United States.

The actual plan was so brief and general that it was almost impossible for anyone to take exception to it. As Acheson later phrased it, "If the Europeans, all or some of them, could get together on a plan of what was needed to get them out of the dreadful situation. . .we would take a look at their plan and see what aid we might practically give."[2]

The Europeans needed no further encouragement. British Foreign Minister Ernest Bevin immediately got in touch with his French counterpart, Georges Bidault. Two weeks later, they met in Paris with Molotov to discuss drawing up a plan. However, Molotov was soon called home. As Bevin commented, his withdrawal "made operations much more simple." By September 1947, the West European nations produced their plan to achieve economic self-sufficiency within four years. They estimated they would need $19.3 billion in U.S. support over that period. The program began in July 1948, continued for three years, and cost the American taxpayer $10.2 billion. By the early 1950s, it had clearly achieved its objectives of reviving the economic life of Western Europe and promoting economic integration within the region.

Acheson returned to private life from July 1947 to the end of 1948. After years of heavy responsibility, he needed a rest and then a change of pace as he resumed the practice of law. However, he was never far from public life in this period. He devoted much of his time to the Citizens' Committee for the Marshall Plan and to the Hoover Commission on the Organization of the Executive Branch of which he was vice chairman. General Marshall and Acheson's successor as Undersecretary, Robert Lovett, took the lead in forming the North Atlantic Treaty Organization and in helping to lay the groundwork for the creation of the Federal Republic of Germany. Acheson became Truman's third Secretary of State in January 1949, in time to complete the NATO treaty and to negotiate the lifting of the Berlin blockade.

Acheson and Asia

Despite his greater interest and competence in European affairs, Acheson was forced to deal mainly with Asian problems during the next four years. President Truman's unexpected victory in the 1948 election coincided with the beginning of the last round in the Chinese civil war.[3] Whole armies of Nationalist troops had begun to desert to the communist side. In January 1949 (the month in which Acheson was confirmed), Mao Tse-tung's forces took Peking. Mao refused to negotiate with his enemy; he demanded Chiang's unconditional surrender. In April, the communist armies crossed the Yangtze River, occupied Nanking, and trapped 300,000 Nationalist soldiers in Shanghai.

Meanwhile, in March, Acheson met with thirty Congressmen who had written to President Truman protesting his "inaction" in China. Acheson told the Congressmen that he could not predict what the administration's next move would be "until some of the dust and smoke of the disaster clears away." This phrase (often shortened to "waiting for the dust to settle") focused the attention of the administration's critics on Acheson personally.[4]

Acheson struggled throughout 1949 to keep the United States' options open; however, two key questions demanded some resolution. Should Washington recognize the communists if they gained control of all or most of China? And in the meantime, was there anything the United States could do to help save the Nationalists from the avalanche of defeat that seemed to be engulfing them? It was easy for Congressional critics to point the finger of blame--but far from likely that they would sanction sending U.S. troops to China.

To try to regain the initiative on these questions, Acheson ordered the State Department's China desk to prepare a "white paper," giving a detailed record of U.S.-Chinese relations in the preceding years.[5] The aim was to demonstrate that Chiang's impending defeat was due to his regime's shortcomings and not the result of anything the United States had done or left undone.

However, the white paper, issued in mid-1949, provoked even sharper attacks on the administration from liberals as well as conservatives. Secretary Acheson's fifteen-page transmittal letter was the most widely read portion of the 1079-page document. (Some Senators condemned the entire paper as biased only hours after it was released.) Even Walter Lippmann critized it as a "self-serving" justification of U.S. policy, which had not been conspicuously successful in the case of China.

Throughout 1949, Acheson tried to keep his options open on the question of recognizing China. At first, he evidently hoped to decide the question according to the traditional Jeffersonian formula.6 However, in June 1949, under pressure from Congressmen who regarded recognition as a form of approval, Acheson promised that the administration would consult Congress before any decision was made.

Meanwhile, unknown to his critics, Secretary Acheson began to explore ways of achieving a goal he shared with them--stopping the spread of communism--without adopting the purely military approach which they seemed to favor. Acheson appointed a special three-man committee to study possible U.S. policy options based on the assumption that "the United States does not intend to permit further extension of communist domination on the continent of Asia or in the Southeast Asia area." However, there is no evidence that Acheson was contemplating anything more than possible economic or military aid to China's neighbors.

In October, Secretary Acheson convened a special meeting of academic specialists on China and leaders in business and other fields. According to the minutes (made public two years later), a "prevailing group" favored recognizing Peking. But former Secretary of State Marshall pointed out that neither Congress nor the American people were ready to support recognition of Peking at that stage. Over the next few months, the Chinese communist government accelerated its campaign of abuse against remaining U.S. officials in China and deliberately destroyed American consular property. Acheson reacted by stating publicly that Peking apparently did not want American recognition.

Believing that they had tied Acheson's hands on the question of recognition, the ctitics of his policy now launched a vigorous campaign to commit the United States to Chiang Kai-shek's support. The Nationalist government and armed forces had just taken refuge on the island of

Taiwan. General MacArthur adopted the view that keeping Taiwan out of communist hands was vital to American security in the western Pacific, reversing his previous position that Taiwan lay outside the American defense perimeter.[7] Former President Hoover and several Republican senators called for various types of U.S. intervention, ranging from "nonmilitary" occupation of Taiwan to naval action in the Taiwan Strait.

At a meeting of the National Security Council, on December 29, 1949, President Truman decided to give no new military support to the Nationalists, although they were allowed to use some unexpended funds from previous aid allotments. The U.S. Joint Chiefs of Staff opposed defending Taiwan if the communists launched an attack. If this happened, the United States would adopt a hands-of attitude toward the fate of the island and the Nationalists. A secret message to all U.S. missions abroad describing this decision was leaked to the press by someone on General MacArthur's staff, creating a furor in Washington. As a result, President Truman announced on January 5, 1950, that the United States would not use its military forces to intervene in the "civil conflict in China," although it would continue to provide Chiang Kai-shek with economic aid.

A week later, Secretary Acheson delivered a speech at the National Press Club in which he described the American defense perimeter in exactly the same terms MacArthur had used the previous March. He was attacked vigorously by his right-wing critics for failing to provide U.S. military guarantees for Taiwan. The same omission of guarantees for South Korea went unnoticed at the time, although Acheson's critics concluded five months later that this had encouraged North Korean's invasion. Acheson's response was that it was only one of many signals sent by both branches of the U.S. government.

If the Russians were watching the United States for signs of our intentions in the Far East, they would have been more impressed by the two years' agitation for withdrawal of combat forces from Korea, the defeat in Congress of a minor aid bill for it, and the increasing discussion of a peace treaty with Japan.[8]

Historians have tended to agree that Acheson was not solely responsible for a U.S. posture that may have encouraged Moscow to support the invasion.[9] The whole history of American actions toward South Korea from 1945 to early 1950 suggested that the United States might not respond if a swift North Korean attack gained control of most of the peninsula. However, the United States, having conquered and occupied South Korea in 1945, was responsible, under international law, for its defense. Moreover, with a growing interest in the stability of Japan, the United States could hardly ignore the likely impact on Japan of a communist invasion of South Korea.

Supporting France in Indochina

Yet even while the Truman administration was striving to retain some flexibility in its China policy, it was moving toward a general anti-communist posture in Asia. The torrent of domestic American criticism unloosed by Chiang's defeat was partially responsible for this new emphasis. Also, the establishment of the NATO alliance in 1949 made it much harder for Acheson to insist (as he had tried to do in the past) on a French pledge of full independence for the Indochina states as a condition for U.S. aid to France. French leaders realized this and adroitly redefined their colonial war as an "anti-communist" struggle.

At the send of 1949, France granted a measure of autonomy (within the French Union) to the Indochina states of Vietnam, Laos, and Cambodia. The United States, in part hoping to broaden their autonomy, established diplomatic relations with the three states in early 1950. But U.S. support of French policy did not stop there. In his memoirs, Acheson notes that:

> During the spring of 1950, after some hesitation, we in the Department recommended aid to France and the Associated States in combating Ho's insurgency, which was backed by the Chinese and Russians. The aid was to be limited to economic and military supplies, stopping short of our own military intervention. If Chinese or Soviet forces should intervene directly, the situation would be considered. The hesitation came from the belief of some of my colleagues that, even with our material and financial help, the French-Bao Dai regime would be defeated in the field by the Soviet- and Chinese-supported Viet Minh. All of us recognized the high probability of this result unless France swiftly transferred authority to the Associated States and organized, trained, and equipped, with our aid, substantial indigenous forces to take over the main burden of the fight.10

Thus, the U.S. aim of moving the Indochinese states toward independence began to give way to the new objective of "containing" Chinese communism. French intelligence reports of a secret military aid agreement between China and Ho Chi Minh's Democratic Republic of Vietnam were made public in the New York Times on May 8, 1950. Reports of this type served the French interest by portraying their war in Indochina as merely one battlefield in the worldwide struggle against communism.

President Truman approved a program of economic and military aid for Indochina in May 1950, and a special technical and economic mission was set up to work directly with the Associated States on economic aid. (The French insisted on retaining full control over all U.S. military aid and most U.S. economic aid destined for Indochina until the end of 1954.) After the start of the Korean war, the American government simply adopted the view that Vietnam and Korea were two fronts of the same war. Keeping France in the war, rather than getting her to grant independence to her colonies, became the main thrust of U.S. policy.

The Korean War Years

During the Korean war, the administration lost much of the freedom of action it had enjoyed since 1945. In part, this reflected the success of American economic initiatives (in which Acheson had played a central role). By the end of 1951, the recovery of our European allies was well on the way to completion; West Germany and Japan were also beginning to resume important roles in world affairs. These former enemy states had developed strong and self-reliant democratic systems. The task of integrating them into our Atlantic and Pactific defense systems was begun by Acheson and carried on by Dulles. Many of our allies and client states gained new influence with Washington during the Korean War-- either because their support was needed in Korea and at the UN or because we could not allow more weak spots to invite Soviet probes.

During the Korean War, there was little likelihood of Acheson (or any other American statesman) improving our relations with China or with the Soviet Union. We were fighting a full scale war with China on the Korean peninsula as well as a diplomatic war at the United Nations.

China's new leaders used the struggle against "American imperialism" to generate mass support for their domestic reforms. Although the United States and Russia were not engaged in a shooting war in this period; Stalin's paranoia had reached an advanced stage; detente was all but impossible.

Acheson as Elder Statesman

Dean Acheson turned sixty in 1953, the year he left public office. His wide interests enabled him to readjust to private life better than most men. For the next eighteen years, he practiced law, traveled, wrote his memoirs and several other important books. During the 1960s, he occasionally donned the mantle of elder statesman, though he would not have cared for the title.

Acheson's close and extraordinarily sucessful relationship with Truman was never equalled with another president. However, the years of service with Truman shaped Acheson's highly positive view of the role of the chief executive. In the 1950s, he sometimes let it be known what he thought of his successor, John Foster Dulles. By his silence, he was kinder to Dean Rusk during his term in office.

Perhaps fearing to be overshadowed, President Kennedy made little use of Acheson's talents. Lyndon Johnson, on the other hand, wanted the support of all elder statesmen (Republican as well as Democrat) who remained in the public eye. He organized them into an informal advisory council, apparently never dreaming they might offer anything but strong support for his Vietnam policy-- as they did until the communist 1968 Tet offensive.

After Tet, Johnson asked Acheson for his views, and Acheson told him he was not sure he had a useful opinion because he had lost faith in the objectivity of the officials who were sent to breif him from time to time. "With all due respect, Mr. President," Acheson was quoted as saying, "the Joint Chiefs of Staff don't know what they're talking about." Johnson said that was a shocking statement. Acheson replied that if it was, perhaps the President ought to be shocked by it.[11]

At Johnson's request, Acheson then spent several weeks reviewing the post-Tet situation with briefing officers from State, Defense, and CIA, whom he selected and cross-examined at his home in Georgetown. On March 15, Acheson gave the President his findings at a somewhat hurried private lunch at the White House. The former Secretary told the President that he was being misled by the Joint Chiefs and that the strategy General Westmoreland was pursuing in Vietnam could not succeed without the application of totally unlimited resources "and maybe five years." He told the President that his recent speeches were unrealistic and the country no longer supported the war. In conclusion, he advised the President to revise his ground strategy, halt or at least greatly reduce the bombing, and liquidate U.S. involvement in the war with the least possible damage to American interests.[12]

Johnson listened to Acheson and did not argue with him. He was undoubtedly shocked by the fact that not only Acheson but most of the other "elder statesmen" advised him to reduce the United States' commitment to Vietnam. All of them, of course, had once favored some form of U.S. involvement. The advice of Acheson and his colleagues seems to have contributed to Johnson's decision to deescalate the war, which he announced two weeks later.

This episode may represent Dean Acheson's chief contribution to American pilicy during the years after he left the State Department. Other major issues that continued to absorb his interest included relations with Germany, southern Africa, nuclear strategy, and international economic policy. Dean Acheson died in October 1971, at a moment when major changes were afoot in these and other key aspects of American policy. It was ironic that President Nixon and Treasury Secretary Connally chose this moment to withdraw U.S. support for aspects of the Bretton Woods system of world economic order. Acheson had been present and very much involved in the creation of a century of unparalleled social and political development.

FOOTNOTES

[1] Dean Acheson, *Present at the Creation: My Years in the State Department* (New York: Norton, 1969), p. 219.

[2] Ibid., p. 234.

[3] The Truman administration had been convinced that America should not intervene directly in the Chinese civil war. However, Secretary Marshall had avoided an open battle with Congress over China policy in order to preserve support for the European recovery program.

[4] Prior to 1949, only a small group of Senators showed any personal animosity toward Acheson. He was confirmed as Secretary by a vote of 83 to 6.

[5] See *United States Relations with China, with Special Reference to the Period 1944-1949*, 2 vols. (Stanford: Stanford University Press, 1968).

[6] Thomas Jefferson held that the United States should recognize any government once it was firmly in control of its national territory and

could be said to represent "the will of the people substantially declared."

[7]The March 2, 1949, New York Times quoted MacArthur as excluding both Korea and Taiwan from U.S. defense perimeter.

[8]Acheson, Present at the Creation, p. 358.

[9]In a June 1970 interview with the author, George Kennan pointed out that internal political pressures in the Soviet Union may have tempted Stalin to launch a diversionary proxy war in 1950. According to Kennan, there was extensive Soviet press commentary on the subject of a U.S.-Japanese security treaty during the first half of 1950--indicating that this subject was being given close attention by Stalin.

[10]Present at the Creation, pp. 672-73.

[11]Townsend Hoopes, The Limits of Power (New York: McKay, 1969), pp. 204-205.

[12]Ibid., p. 205.

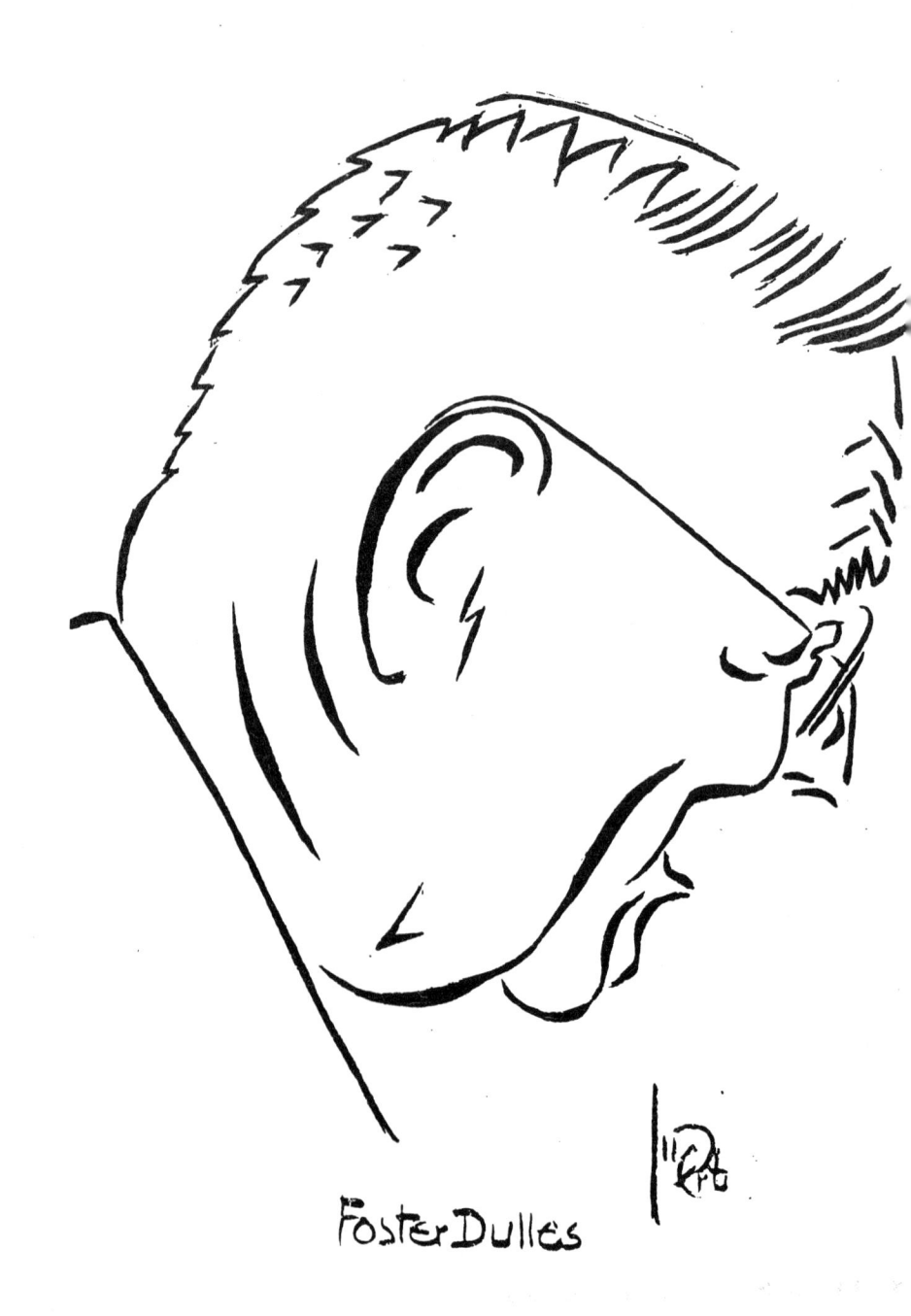

Foster Dulles

Chapter 5

JOHN FOSTER DULLES: HARD-LINER

OR TIGHTROPE-WALKER?

In April 1950, Dean Acheson added to his inner circle of advisors a leading spokesman of the Republican party's moderate wing. To help preserve a bipartisan consensus for administration policy, John Foster Dulles became Acheson's special assistant.[1] In this role, Dulles negotiated the Japanese Peace Treaty, perhaps the greatest achievement of his career. His views at the time were not far removed from those of Truman or Acheson. For example, he had just published a book, War or Peace, in which he favored admitting China to the United Nations if she met her international obligations.

Dulles left the Truman administration in time to take part in the 1952 election campaign. With the aim of being nominated Secretary of State, he began to advocate "liberation" of countries under communist control, though he implied this could be done mainly by propaganda. To foreign diplomats, it was never clear whether Dulles's statements should be taken at face value or discounted as political rhetoric.

In retrospect, it seems plain that he was positioning himself as Ike's indispensable aide in dealing with a conservative Congress and with foreign client states. On broad policy, he invariably deferred to the president, whose instincts and rhetoric were more liberal.

In May 1952, Dulles visited Eisenhower at his NATO headquarters and showed him an article which he was about to publish in Life magazine.[2] His thesis was that the Truman administration's strategy of containment was not designed to reduce or eliminate the communist threat to the free world; it merely aimed at making it possible to live with the threat. Dulles argued that containment required "gigantic military expenditures [which] unbalance our budget and require taxes so heavy that they discourage incentive." Besides, "this concentration on military matters...transfers from the civilian to the military decisions which profoundly affect our domestic life and our foreign relations."

How could the United States reduce its defense budget and at the same time gain greater security? Dulles proposed a new strategy that seemed to rely almost entirely on a willingness to use nuclear weapons wherever U.S. interests were threatened:

> There is one solution and only one: that is for the free world to develop the will and organize the means to retaliate instantly against open aggression by Red armies, so that, if it occurred anywhere, we could and would strike back where it hurts by means of our choosing.

Dulles did not stop at hinting at nuclear retaliation against any and all Soviet offensive moves. He also urged the United States to roll back the Russian gains in Eastern Europe. Soviet leaders have trampled on the "moral or natural law," he said; "for that violation they can and should be made to pay." The United States must let it be known that "it wants and expects liberation to occur," for that would give hope to captive peoples and "put heavy new burdens on the jailers." He insisted that this was not a call for "a series of bloody uprisings and reprisals." But he did not specify how liberation should be achieved--except to urge that the Voice of America and Radio Free Europe concentrate their programs on this theme.

General Eisenhower wrote Dulles, shortly after his visit to NATO headquarters, thanking him for his article and saying he was "as deeply impressed as ever with the directness and simplicity of your approach to complex problems." This comment may have been slightly tongue-in-cheek. To his old friend, General Lucius Clay, Eisenhower wrote that he agreed with the idea of retaliation where a vital U.S. interest such as Berlin was at state. But

> . . .what should we do if Soviet political agression. . .successively chips away exposed portions of the free world? So far as our resulting economic situation is concerned, such an eventuality would be just as bad for us as if the area had been captured by force. To my mind, this is a case where the theory of "retaliation" falls down.[3]

Dulles performed the difficult task of writing the foreign policy planks for the 1952 Republican platform. These had to be acceptable to both the Taft and Eisenhower wings of the party, whose views were often diametrically opposed. Dulles's planks resolved this problem by attacking the Democrats for abandoning the peoples of Eastern Europe to Soviet domination. The GOP platform promised to repudiate the Yalta agreements and any others which "aid communist enslavements." The platform pledged that "we shall again make liberty into a beacon light of hope that will. . . mark the end of the negative, futile, and immoral policy of 'containment.'"

"Liberation" was the theme of Dulles's campaign speeches on behalf of General Eisenhower. Although Eisenhower himself had reservations about using this theme, it probably helped to draw together the two main wings of the Republican party. After Eisenhower's landslide election, Taft and other conservatives supported Dulles's nomination as secretary of state. Dulles, in return, consistently sought their advice on foreign policy.

Truce in Korea

General Eisenhower promised during the campaign to go to Korea if he were elected. In December 1952, he redeemed the pledge and then issued a brief statement urging the opposing side to accept an honorable settlement. In Eisenhower's view, they would do so only if they were convinced the United States was prepared to use more force to achieve this result. Therefore, shortly after his inauguration, he sent more U.S. aircraft to South Korea, made public a plan to enlarge the South Korean Army, and placed nuclear missiles on Okinawa. He also "unleashed" Chiang Kai-shek's forces by canceling orders to the Seventh Fleet to prevent their return to the mainland of China.

It is, of course, impossible to know just what effect these moves produced on Chinese and North Korean leaders. In any case, American pressure was probably reinforced by Soviet advice. Stalin died in March 1953, and his place was taken by a group of younger leaders. Some of them could see the advantage to Russia of "peaceful coexistence" with the West.

On March 28, the Chinese government agreed to an exchange of sick and wounded prisoners, and China then announced that prisoners unwilling to return to their native land could be handed over to a neutral state.

However, the hardest task was to persuade our Asian clients to accept a political settlement; this was a major challenge for Dulles. South Korean President Syngman Rhee refused to sign a truce without an American pledge to resume the war unless Korea were unified in ninety days. President Eisenhower rejected this condition as wholly unjustified and unrealistic. Attempts to console the Korean leader with offers of a U.S. security treaty, economic aid and diplomatic support all failed. After the United States signed a prisoner exchange agreement, Rhee freed twenty-seven thousand North Korean prisoners who refused repatriation. The time had come for the Eisenhower administration to deal firmly with its Asian client.

Dulles sent Assistant Secretary of State Walter Robertson to Seoul. For two weeks, Robertson allowed the autocratic Korean leader to blow off steam; then he politely but firmly urged him to cease sabotaging the negotiations, trust Eisenhower and Dulles and allow the armistice to go into effect. Next, Robertson, Dulles and Eisenhower all applied themselves to the task of persuading the conservative wing in Congress that the armistice agreement was in the U.S. interest.[4] To mollify potential critics, Washington issued a warning (in the name of all UN members with troops in South Korea) that renewed aggression in Korea might lead to retaliatory action beyond that country's borders. These combined efforts produced success.

Dulles and Indochina

The Korean truce in 1953 released the French government from its pledge to continue the war in Indochina as long as American forces were fighting in Korea. Ironically, Secretary Dulles had become more committed to the Indochina war than France was. Dulles deplored the speed with which French leaders made contact with Ho Chi Minh and tried to open negotiations. However, in February 1954, the Big Four foreign ministers agreed (over Dulles's initial objection) to convene a meeting of all the parties to the Indochina and Korean wars, including China.

Meanwhile, the French chose the untenable site of Dien Bien Phu for a climactic battle, which served to dramatize their plight on the eve of the conference.

Dulles sought repeatedly to stave off what he considered a disastrous defeat for the free world by organizing a joint Anglo-American-French commitment to defend Indochina.[5] President Eisenhower ruled that the United States would not intervene without a congressional declaration of war--and then only if Britain would join the effort and if France would grant its Indochinese colonies full independence. France seemed willing to meet the final condition, but neither Congress nor the British government was willing to support Dulles's policy of "united action."

Dulles distinguished himself at Geneva by a public display of rudeness to China's Premier Chou En-lai, with whom he refused even to shake hands. He adopted a generally obstructive attitude, even after a surprisingly lenient agreement emerged that would limit the area of communist control to North Vietnam and two provinces of Laos. To Eden, Dulles seemed more concerned with playing up to the China bloc in Congress than with helping France extricate herself from a hopeless colonial war. Finally, Eden, Churchill, Eisenhower and Dulles met in Washington and it was arranged that Dulles's deputy, General Walter Bedell Smith, would announce that the United States would not use force to upset the agreements that had been reached.

Quemoy and Matsu

Dulles's approach to China policy remained highly ambiguous, though he seemed to believe until his death that a hard-line position was required by domestic politics and the need for world order. Eisenhower, who might have overruled him on this issue, did not. However, he may have helped prevent the situation from growing worse.

The Geneva conference on Indochina was followed by a series of crises over two small islands, Quemoy and Matsu, located only a few miles from the China mainland. Chiang Kai-shek professed to need the islands for his planned reconquest of China. He occupied the islands, and the Chinese Communists subjected them to periodic artillery barrages. Both sides evidently sought to test Soviet and American willingness to intervene in the western Pacific.

The situation offered a wide range of possibilities. Most of America's allies hoped that Eisenhower would see the futility of giving Chiang further support and that he would opt for normal relations with Peking. Conversely, there was a danger of war between Chinese Communist and American forces if the United States went to extremes in backing the Nationalist position.

Eisenhower decided that the United States would not risk war by using force to protect the offshore islands. This condition was spelled out in a December 1954 defense agreement between the Chinese Nationalist and American governments. The agreement was supplemented by an exchange of notes in which the Nationalists renounced the right to use force (clearly meaning against the China mainland) without U.S. concurrence. Dulles carried out these sensitive negotiations, which sharply limited U.S. military support to Chiang.

Detente with the USSR?

The broadest foreign policy challenge faced by the Eisenhower administration was the rise of Khrushchev and his campaign for "peaceful coexistence" with the West. This coincided with evidence of rapid Soviet military and economic progress. However, like many Americans, Dulles simply refused to acknowledge that the Soviet system might be evolving under new leadership. He discounted Khrushchev's achievements in the domestic sphere, such as the reduction of police terror and a partial success in rationalizing agriculture. To have acknowledged these improvements would have meant, in Dulles's view, conceding that the moral gap between Russia and the United States was narrowing. When Khrushchev began to imitate the American programs of military and economic aid, Dulles condemned as "immoral" the neutralist leaders who accepted aid from both superpowers.

The Soviet government used its growing affluence to attain a rough strategic balance with the United States. Eisenhower and other liberal statemen of the free world saw this as a potentially hopeful development, since it made the use of strategic nuclear weapons unthinkable. Dulles seemed to disagree. He continued to speak as if it was possible to use America's nuclear arsenal to "roll back" communist territorial gains.

However, Khrushchev had his problems too. His denunciation of Stalin and his modifications of Stalin's domestic and foreign policy led to serious tensions within the communist world by the end of 1956. Soviet leaders had to cope with dissident students, accept a new Polish government of less certain loyalty to Moscow, and send tanks to suppress a major rebellion in Hungary. The United States made no move to support the Hungarians, thus demonstrating that Dulles's talk of "liberation" was mere rhetoric.

Chinese leaders saw in Khrushchev's policy of "peaceful coexistence" with the West a likelihood of reduced Soviet political and military support for China. This became, in a sense, a self-fulfilling prophecy. It was not long, therefore, before Maoism was being proclaimed in China as the orthodox branch of Leninism, and Moscow and Peking were in open competition for political influence in the communist "bloc" and in the Third World.

While Dulles persisted in viewing the communist world as monolithic, Eisenhower was more optimistic about the prospects for Soviet-American detente. He probably sensed that the United States would forfeit much of its remaining world influence unless it explored the possibilities for reducing East-West tensions.

Eisenhower and Dulles at Geneva

In 1955, the British Conservative government proposed an East-West summit conference at Geneva. Eisenhower, over Dulles's objections, agreed to attend. In briefing memoranda prior to the summit, Dulles warned Eisenhower that one of the main reasons the Soviets wanted the meeting was to project the "appearance that the West conceded the Soviet rulers a moral and social equality which will help maintain their satellite rule by disheartening potential resistance." Dulles urged the president to avoid social meetings at Geneva where he would be photographed with the Soviet leaders and to maintain "an austere counternance on occasions where photographing is inevitable."[6]

Despite these warnings, Eisenhower allowed his smile and his basic optimism to shine through in public statements immediately prior to the summit. The reason he was going to Geneva, he announced, was "to change the spirit that has characterized the intergovernmental relationships of the world during the past ten years." This was what most people wanted to hear. Even Dulles was not immune to the natural impulse to look for some easing of world tensions; at the public celebration of the Austrian peace treaty in May 1955, he repeatedly shook hands with Molotov and even embraced him and professed to see in the withdrawal of Soviet occupation troops from Austria "something contagious."

The summit conference at Geneva in July 1955 was the first East-West meeting of the heads of government since the start of the cold war. The agenda items included German reunification and European security, disarmament, and development of East-West contacts. As expected, none of these important issues were resolved. However, the meeting was widely hailed as marking the emergence of Eisenhower and Khrushchev as major statesmen who accepted the balance of power and hoped to reduce world tensions. President Eisenhower surprised his colleagues by proposing an exchange of data on military installations by the major powers. The idea was not pursued at the time, in part because none of the delegations had the necessary technical specialists.

In their public comments on the summit, the Western leaders each struck a positive note, claiming that all the major powers now saw that nuclear war was inconceivable. Only Dulles seemed to concentrate on dampening the euphoria. At a press conference, he said it was "premature" to talk about an "era of good feelings" between East and West.

In a secret cable to American ambassadors abroad, Dulles acknowledged that Geneva had created certain problems for the free world, which had been held together for the past eight years "largely by a cement compounded of fear and a sense of moral superiority." He called the Soviets' peace offensive a tactical maneuver forced upon them by their comparatively weak economic and military position. Although he expressed hope that this Soviet tactic might "assume the force of an irreversible trend," he pointed out that the U.S. government "does not acquiesce in the present power position of the Soviet Union in Europe."

The 1956 Suez Crisis

Ironically, just one year later, Dulles's own maneuvering through the maze of Middle Eastern interests and rivalries placed the United States and the Soviet Union side by side in opposition to Britain, France, and Israel. The 1956 Suez crisis emphasized several points, none of them reassuring from the American standpoint. First, the interests of the United States and those of its major allies were not always the same or easily reconciled. Second, the Soviet Union could and would use military aid (a familiar American device) to extend its influence into strategically important Third World countries. Finally, neutralist leaders such as Nasser saw nothing "immoral" about accepting Soviet aid, and they believed they could do so without opening their countries to Soviet subversion.

In early 1956, Nasser tried to assure his leadership of the Arab world by asking each of the major powers for military aid. All except Russia either stalled or refused him outright. A Soviet-Egyptian arms agreement was then reached. Czechoslovakia was the official supplier, to make the agreement seem less provocative to the West.

On July 19, 1956, Secretary Dulles reacted to Nasser's closer ties with Russia by withdrawing an earlier pledge to help finance the Aswan dam, Egypt's major economic development project. Nasser had hinted that the Soviets were willing to finance the whole Aswan project and that he would accept the Soviet offer unless the United States and Britain increased their contributions. Dulles believed the Soviets would be unable to make good their offer. By withdrawing the American pledge to finance any part of Aswan, he thought that he was calling Moscow's bluff. At the same time, he meant to show neutralist leaders everywhere that "free world" states had first claim on U.S. aid funds.

Nasser responded by nationalizing the Suez Canal, which had been run by an international company. His right to do so was firmly based on international law, provided he allowed all powers equal access to the waterway. However, British, French, and Israeli leaders did not trust Nasser. They secretly planned an attack aimed at wresting the canal from his hands and overthrowing him.

Britain saw this as the key to its continued influence in the region. France believed Nasser's support was keeping alive that Algerian insurrection. Israel sought to cut Egypt's military aid links with Russia. Dulles, unaware of the planned intervention, tried to mediate the Suez Canal dispute, but he found it difficult to conceal his own distrust of Nasser, which undermined whatever credibility his mediation might have had.

In October, Israeli, British and French forces attacked, but they failed to seize the canal before Nasser blocked it by sinking some ships. Dulles intervened and threatened to forbid exports of oil to Britain unless it withdrew its forces. The British were temporarily dependent on oil from America to replace Middle Eastern sources that were closed to them.

Thus, the U.S. action was decisive in ending the short war. However, the United States gained little political credit to offset this severe blow to three important allies. Khrushchev reaped a great propaganda victory in Afro-Asian countries by threatening Britain, France, and Israel with rocket attacks unless they withdrew their forces--after they had already decided to do so.

The American Leadership Crisis

The Suez fiasco was symptomatic of America's weakening in the late 1950s. Stalin's ruthlessness had made him the ideal enemy against whom to mobilize the free world. Dulles found it extremely difficult to adapt to the more subtle challenges of Khrushchev.

In retrospect, the Eisenhower administration's most creative step in foreign affairs may have been its participation in the 1955 Geneva conference. This opened the way to further relaxation of cold war tensions. However, President Eisenhower suffered his first heart attack in September 1955; after he recovered, he was inclined to leave the conduct of foreign affairs even more to others.

Dulles served as the active manager of U.S. foreign policy until shortly before he died from cancer in May 1959. (Dulles suffered his first attack of cancer, and was partially cured, shortly after the Suez crisis in 1956.) During these years, he exercised his gift for tactical maneuver, improvising a series of separate responses to crises but seldom seizing the initiative or settling in motion any long-range policies. More and more, his purpose seemed to be to maintain close relations with America's allies and client states that ringed the Sino-Soviet bloc. Dulles ignored the increasing groundswell of criticism, at home and abroad, of his hostile attitude toward China and Russia. In the eyes of a growing number of people, the onus for continuing cold war tensions lay mainly with the United States.

Dulles had two main strengths as a diplomat. He exercised close control over the whole range of U.S. agencies engaged in foreign affairs, and he sometimes displayed great skill at hedging his commitments. After Dulles's death, no one asserted the same type of control over U.S. foreign policy for about three years, until the Kennedy administration passed through the fires of the Curban missile crisis.

Eisenhower and Dulles proved to be a remarkably effective team--even after ill health struck them both. Ike set the broad limits of continuity and change in U.S. policy--sometimes but by no means always rejecting his secretary's judgment. Dulles knew how to extract the last ounce of cooperation from the "primitives" in Congress and from the growing ranks of U.S. client states abroad. Yet in his final years, he was crippled not only by cancer but also by his inability to deal as effectively with our major allies, who had regained their prewar strength and self-confidence.

FOOTNOTES

[1] Senator Arthur Vandenberg was probably the first to suggest using Dulles in this role, but Dean Rusk and Walton Butterworth (the incoming and outgoing heads of the Asian bureau) were also involved in the appointment. John M. Allison assisted Dulles in the treaty negotiations, and then served briefly as head of the bureau before taking charge of the embassy in Japan.

[2] John Foster Dulles, "A Policy of Boldness," Life, May 19, 1952, Vol. 32, pp. 146-160.

[3] See Townsend Hoopes, The Devil and John Foster Dulles (Boston: Little Brown, 1973), pp. 128-129. Eisenhower never resolved this issue in his own mind during his eight years as president. He told his successor, John F. Kennedy, that he preferred to leave all options open to him for dealing with the 1960-61 crisis in Laos.

[4] Dulles had put Robertson (a conservative Democrat who had served in China) in charge of Far Eastern affairs at the suggestion of members on the congressional "China bloc," with whom Dulles wanted to maintain good relations.

[5] At one stage, Dulles and Admiral Radford, chairman of the Joint Chiefs of Staff, proposed a U.S. bombing attack against Viet Minh bases near Dien Bien Phu.

[6] Dulle's memorandum to Eisenhower, June 18, 1955, contained in the Dulles papers at the Princeton University Library.

Dean Rusk

Chapter 6

DEAN RUSK: CONTAINING COMMUNISM IN ASIA

In 1949, shortly after Mao Tse-tung's victory in China, Dean Rusk did something few people would ordinarily do. He volunteered for a demotion. He was forty years old at the time, and he had been promoted twice within the year, first to assistant secretary of state and then to deputy undersecretary. However, the Truman administration was under intense partisan attack because of its China policy. Some of the heat was directed at Walton Butterworth, a career officer who was in charge of the Far Eastern Bureau. Rusk volunteered to take charge of the bureau, which meant returning to the rank of assistant secretary.

The gesture reflected a sense of duty and a sense of decency toward colleagues. Rusk believed that it was unfair to let a career FSO be exposed to such intense political pressure. More than that, he could see that the main focus of U.S. policy was shifting toward Asia. What sort of man was this who so plainly enjoyed dealing with tough problems under enormous pressure?

Dean Rusk was born in 1909 in Georgia. His father was forced by a throat ailment to leave the ministry and earn a living as a small farmer and mail-carrier. Rusk worked his way through Davidson College in North Carolina and won a Rhodes Scholarship to Oxford, where he received an Honours degree in 1934. He then taught at Mills College in California and served as dean of the faculty before World War II cut short his academic career. He was called to active duty as an Army officer in 1940 and saw service in the China-Burma-India theater, before joining the State Department in 1946.

International law and organization were among Rusk's main interests, and he was named Assistant Chief of the International Organization division. However, his decision to seek the Asian bureau assignment did not reflect a sharp change from one area of specialization to another. His strengths were always those of a generalist who could immerse himself in any important problem or crisis. Moreover, he had been interested in Asia since his student years, and much of his public life would be concerned with Asian affairs.

Rusk's offer to take charge of the Far Eastern Bureau at this time was seen as an act of courage by his superiors, and it earned him a lasting debt of gratitude. In 1960, President-elect Kennedy asked a number of senior Democrats (and some Republicans) whom they would suggest as Secretary of State. Rusk's name appeared on many of the lists that were submitted. He was still unknown to the general public, at this stage, and also to most of President Kennedy's close associates. Would he have been offered the job if it were widely known that he had been one of the architects of the China containment policy?

During the spring of 1950, as Senator Joseph McCarthy began attacking the State Department for being "soft on communism," two decisions were made that would help transform U.S. Far Eastern policy. Secretary Acheson decided to send military aid to the French forces in Indochina, and he invited John Foster Dulles to join the administration. It is unlikely that Rusk had much to do with the first decision, because Indochina was a French colony and remained the responsibility of the European Bureau. However, Rusk was among those with whom Acheson discussed the decision to invite Dulles to be his special assistant.

The Korean War began just a few weeks after Dulles reported for duty. In retrospect, Dulles and Rusk both seem to have concluded almost immediately that the administration must move toward open confrontation with China. This represented a change of public posture for Dulles, who had previously sounded a more conciliatory note.

Dean Rusk, on the other hand, had not been identified with the subject of China policy before the North Korean invasion. Yet he played a central role in shaping the administration response to that event. He was among the first officials to discuss the attack with Secretary Acheson and to suggest going to the United Nations for a mandate. His expertise in UN affairs and a recent clash with Congress over aid to Korea may have influenced the fateful decision not to seek a Congressional declaration of war. This left Congress free to attack administration policy, since it had never gone on record as favoring U.S. intervention. Moreover, the precedent of not seeking a formal declaration of war was followed by President Johnson in Vietnam in 1964-65.

Rusk also supported the idea of moving the Seventh Fleet into the Taiwan Strait and trying to isolate China politically and economically. Though he was not the author of these ideas, which had been debated by Congress for some months, he was very much involved in the task of building a new domestic foreign policy consensus. Rusk testified vigorously before Congress and in other public forums on the need to "contain" China. His statements were couched in the same exagerated rhetoric China was directing at America. For example, he called the Chinese Communist regime a "colonial Russian government--a Slavic Manchukuo on a larger scale." If these polemics reduced partisan pressure on the administration, the price was great: twenty years of inflexibility in U.S. policy toward China.

Rusk remained in charge of the Asian Bureau during the hottest part of the Korean War, until the end of 1951. Throughout this period, he steadfastly supported the view that China was

the aggressor and must be treated as such by
the United States and the United Nations. Kennan
and others who were close to the situation have
claimed that this hard-line approach caused
the Truman administration to spurn Chinese peace
feelers during 1950 and after. Many writers
believe the administration allowed itself to
be forced by Congressional pressure to adopt a
China policy which they could not justify on its
merits.1

    Rusk and Dulles both left the State
Department in early 1952, after the Japanese
Peace Treaty was safely through the Senate.
Before leaving the Department, Rusk negotiated
the long and complex Administrative Agreement
which was appended to the U.S.-Japan Security
Treaty. It covered the status of U.S. forces
in Japan and related matters and helped to set
the tone of U.S.-Japanese relations over the
next twenty years. This is one of the principal
treaties that Rusk negotiated personally, and
like so many other U.S. treaties of the Cold
War period, it took the form of an executive
agreement.

    With this work done, Rusk assumed his new
position as President of the Rockefeller
Foundation, where he remained until 1960.
He thoroughly enjoyed the new job, and he made
no effort to publicize his foreign policy views
during this nine-year period. Dulles
consulted him occasionally, but if they considered an opening to China they must have
concluded that the climate was not ripe.
Indeed, Dulles even intensified the military
containment of China through the organization
of SEATO. In any case, by the end of the
decade, very few people associated Rusk with
U.S. policy toward China. Nor did they
associate him with Dulles, who was regarded by
many Americans as the main author of the anti-
Mao dogma.

When John F. Kennedy was elected President, he deliberately passed over several senior Democrats, such as Adlai Stevenson, and chose Dean Rusk as his Secretary of State. Rusk helped to balance the image of an administration composed of bright but inexperienced academics getting their first taste of the world of politics. Rusk was a reassuring presence--sound, steady, well-versed in the ways of Washington. At fifty-two, he was also a good deal older than the President or his immediate circle.

Averell Harriman, who was a generation older than Rusk, began as an outsider in the Kennedy administration and soon became one of its key figures, rising to the rank of undersecretary for political affairs. Rusk and Harriman do not seem to have been rivals; they respected each other for their abilities. When Harriman took charge of the Asian Bureau in late 1961, Rusk told him to make any decision he felt "comfortable" about making at the bureau level.

Though Rusk failed to caution Kennedy against the Bay of Pigs invasion plan, which they inherited from the previous administration, Rusk survived the shake-up of Kennedy's senior staff which followed this disaster. However, the president did place a number of his close associates in the State Department, hoping to make it more responsive to his ideas and orders. From the White House, it appeared that many career officials were inclined to ignore the administration's policy whenever it suited them. (Kennedy had been taught by his father to be suspicious of diplomats; the elder Kennedy felt he was snubbed by his own staff when he served as Ambassador to London). In effect President Kennedy became his own secretary of state.

Though most of the New Frontiersmen were relative newcomers to foreign affirs, this made them all the more anxious to develop a distinctive style or image for the administration.

John Foster Dulles was a convenient symbol, exactly what they wanted the public to believe they were not. While many of his policies went unchanged, Dulles himself was vilified as old, devious, intolerant of African and Asian neutralists, inflexible in his dealings with the communist powers, and a one-man State Department.

No one accused Rusk, at least initially, of sharing these qualities. The White House would have welcomed more leadership by Rusk, provided he did not undercut the President. In fact, he soon began to carve out a place for himself as a private counselor to President Kennedy. After the Bay of Pigs fiasco and the unsuccessful summit with Khrushchev in Vienna, Kennedy paid more attention to Rusk's advice. From the limited sources available such as the Pentagon Papers, it appears that Rusk had a penchant for urging the president to steer a middle course between the views offered by various departments, including at times his own.

Some of Rusk's associates in the Department were concerned about his failure to take the lead on Indochina policy during his first year in office. The reasons for this are unclear, though it may be significant that the war had not yet reached the stage of open crisis. In Laos, however, events in 1961 forced the Kennedy administration to make a basic decision. U.S. policy toward that kingdom was in chaos, with the Pentagon and State Department supporting two rival Lao armies and political factions. A third group, openly backed by Hanoi and Moscow, was on the verge of military victory. President Kennedy decided to seek an agreement with the Soviets to avoid major power involvement in the war.

Rusk dutifully explained the plan for neutralizing Laos to Thai leaders at a SEATO conference in Bangkok. He failed to convince them that it would help stablize the region, perhaps he was not very optimistic on this score himself. Averell Harriman, who held the rank of ambassador-at-large, took charge of the issue and within a few months had reached agreement with the Soviets. He then persuaded the Lao political factions to form a neutral coalition government. Harriman's conduct at the 1962 Geneva conference, at which these accords were signed, contrasted sharply with Dulles's negative behavior at the 1954 Geneva conference. However, Thai leaders remained skeptical; they preferred direct U.S. military involvement of the sort that helped prevent communist forces from overrunning Laos until 1975.

Meanwhile, Secretary of Defense Robert McNamara, General Maxwell Taylor, and Vice President Johnson all visited Saigon during 1961 and came home recommending greatly increased U.S. support for Diem's regime. Younger and more liberal friends of the President tended to emphasize the weakness of Diem's political support. Rusk cast himself in the role of a moderator, urging a gradual rather than sudden increase in U.S. aid.

In the summer of 1962, the administration's policy toward Indochina began to harden. Pentagon criticism of the Laotian accords may have triggered the change. The World Court also decided a Thai-Khmer border dispute in Cambodia's favor; both nations responded to the news by preparing for war. When Cambodia's chief of State, Prince Sihanouk, demanded a U.S. guarantee of his borders, as in Laos, he was flatly refused.

The Kennedy administration's tacit formula, which may have been suggested by Rusk, was to balance the neutralization of Laos with a tougher stand in Cambodia and Vietnam. The President was concerned not only about grumbling within the Pentagon but also about a growing nervousness among the leaders of Thailand and other U.S.

client states in Asia. Secretary Rusk wrote a memorandum to the Thai Foreign Minister, Thanat Khoman, expressing U.S. support for the kingdom's security. The administration also began a massive military build-up in Thailand. This helped reassure Thai leaders in Bangkok, but it also invited North Vietnam and China to increase their subversive pressures.

Meanwhile in Vietnam, President Diem and his family had failed to consolidate their political position. They were becoming more and more obsessed with fear of disloyalty — in the government, the army, and the Buddhist clergy.

Within the U.S. executive branch, it was widely recognized that Diem's paranoia was undermining what little political support he had. American officials were divided over whether the United States should cut its losses or move in and take charge of the war. Not all U.S. military leaders favored the latter approach; those who did wanted a quick, all-out effort with no political constraints such as those that were applied during the Korean War.

Vice President Johnson, General Taylor and Secretary McNamara all appeared to be lining up behind this approach during 1962. Rusk probably scaled down their most extreme proposals. One reason, undoubtedly, was that he was more aware of the political risks of moving ahead when U.S. public opinion had not been prepared for all-out war in Indochina.

During 1963, Diem's position deteriorated steadily as Vietnamese Buddhists launched a campaign against his pro-Catholic policies. The liberal wing of the Kennedy administration saw this as an appropriate moment to disengage American support from Diem; by late summer, President Kennedy publicly stated that Diem must reform his regime or risk losing U.S. aid. Republican Henry Cabot Lodge was recruited as

Ambassador to Saigon; the administration seemed to be trying to lay a basis of bi-partisan support for its as yet unstated goals. Behind the scenes, Rusk, Johnson, and Secretary McNamara all resisted the idea of abandoning Diem and South Vietnam. However, in early November, Diem and his brother Nhu were murdered by ambitious officers of their own army. General Minh then formed the first of a series of unstable military governments.

At this time, certain members of the Kennedy administration had also begun to re-examine the policy of "containing" China. Assistant Secretary of State Roger Hilsman assigned his deputy, Marshall Green, to prepare plans for opening a "civil dialogue" with Peking. Key figures in the administration, including Dean Rusk, tended to take sides on the China issue in much the same way that they were split on Indochina. This was hardly surprising. The subjects of China and Indochina had been intertwined in U.S. policy for over twenty years, and they have remained hard to disentangle even after our disengagement from Vietnam.

On November 22, 1963, President Kennedy was assassinated. He had not yet decided what to do about China or post-Diem Indochina. However, his successor, Lyndon Johnson, and the key advisors whom he inherited (including Secretary Rusk) were already in basic agreement. The Pentagon Papers note that Johnson signed a classified memorandum, four days after President Kennedy's death, stating that it was U.S. policy to help the people and government of South Vietnam "to win their contest against the externally directed and supported communist conspiracy."

A number of liberals who had been close to President Kennedy and who favored a neutralist solution in Vietnam left the government or were given assignments unrelated to Indochina. The idea of a "dialogue" with China was also shelved by Rusk. He replaced Assistant Secretary Hilsman with William Bundy, whose brother remained as National Security Advisor. General Taylor was named Ambassador to Saigon, and a small group of State, Defense, and CIA officials were put to work secretly drafting contingency plans for major U.S. military intervention.

In the summer of 1964, McNamara rather than Rusk took the lead within the administration in seeking passage of the Tonkin Gulf resolution. This authorized the President to take "all necessary measures to repel any armed attack against the forces of the United States and to prevent further aggression." At this point in the war, there were 16,000 U.S. troops in Vietnam and 163 Americans had died in the line of duty. It would still have been possible for the administration to disengage U.S. forces from the war. However, each American casualty seemed to strengthen the hand of those who favored intervention and weakened those who wanted to withdraw.

Johnson's action in the Tonkin Gulf incident was widely supported at the time in U.S. public opinion polls and editorials as well as by Congress. In the fall 1964 election campaign, Johnson said "we have tried very carefully to restrain ourselves and not to enlarge the (Vietnam) War." He said he was opposed to sending American boys to fight "a war that I think ought to be fought by the boys of Asia to help protect their own land."

Nevertheless, the Pentagon Papers provide evidence that Rusk and other key advisors to the President were convinced throughout 1964 that large-scale U.S. intervention would be necessary unless the Saigon government somehow pulled itself together. The President was inexperienced in foreign affairs and inclined to concentrate on the election, though his victory had hardly been in doubt since Goldwater's nomination. The secret decision to bomb Vietnam was made less than a month after the election.

Rusk supported the bombing and apparently did not advise seeking a formal declaration of war, but he pointed out that the United States would be blamed much more if it tried and failed to save South Vietnam by bombing than if it did not try at all. Therefore, he strongly urged the President to explain publicly the reasons for intervention before escalating the war. Johnson overruled him, preferring to announce this major new foreign policy decision after events had already been set in motion. It would then take a massive, and unprecedented groundswell of public opposition to reverse it.[2]

This became the pattern for the Johnson administration's conduct of foreign affairs: secret planning within a very small circle of advisers, followed by dramatic announcements of decisions while they were being carried out. As the war progressed and the American public became more divided, Johnson and his senior advisors deliberately restricted the flow of information about what options were being considered to a smaller and smaller group of executive branch officials. Since many Indochina specialists within the government were suspected of favoring U.S. disengagement from Vietnam, they were isolated from the policy-making process, much as the State Department's China specialists were isolated or fired in the 1950's.

Johnson and McNamara both believed that the bombing raids would force hanoi to negotiate. It is uncertain whether Rusk shared this view before the raids began. Like many U.S. military experts, he may have doubted from the start that gradually increasing pressure in the air war and ground war would succeed. The Vietnamese communists had outlasted the French, and they were willing to bear a far higher rate of casualties than Americans would accept for a cause they did not understand. Rusk realized this more clearly than Johnson or his other key advisors. Yet he told the Senate Foreign Relations Committee in 1966:[3]

> The heart of the problem in South Vietnam is the effort of North Vietnam to impose its will by force. For that purpose, Hanoi had infiltrated into South Vietnam large quantities of arms and tens of thousands of trained and armed men, including units of the North Vietnamese Regular Army. It is that external aggression, which the north has repeatedly escalated, that is responsible for the presence of U.S. combat forces. . . .
> The United States has a clear and direct commitment to the security of South Vietnam against external attack. The integrity of our commitments is absolutely essential to the preservation of peace right around the globe.
> At stake also is the still broader question whether aggression is to be permitted once again to succeed. We know from painful experience that aggression feeds on aggression. . . .
> We have tried to make it clear over and over again that, although Hanoi is the prime actor in this situation, it is the policy of Peking that has greatly stimulated Hanoi and has apparently blocked the path toward a conference.

Very few Congressmen were willing to accept the onus for attacking the Commander-in-Chief while U.S. forces were in danger. Some who did lost their seats in Congress

Because of the high stakes involved, Rusk evidently felt justified in resisting efforts by various parties to mediate the war. The first person to attempt mediation was U Thant, the U.N. Secretary-General; this was followed by an Italian government effort in 1965. Rusk may have believed that mediation leading to a neutralist regime in Saigon would look to most of the world like a victory for Hanoi. On more than one occasion, the administration upset peace-making efforts by escalating the war. These episodes quickly became known (and generated opposition to U.S. policy at home and abroad) because of the large numbers of journalists covering the war and because journalists were sometimes actively involved in the peace initiatives.

One aspect of Rusk's approach which clearly hearkened back to the Korean War was his effort to persuade allied governments to enter the struggle. In the Vietnam War, this met with minimal success. Thailand became our most active and exposed ally; her contributions were not limited to sending troops but also included use of her territory to mount the air war and other military operations against Vietnam. The result was to make Thailand a prime target for Vietnamese and Chinese subversion and to place her in a very delicate position when the U.S. began to withdraw from the war in 1968.

Korea, Australia, New Zealand, and the Philippines also sent units which took part in the war and which they later withdrew after the U.S. began to disengage. Each of these countries found it difficult to adjust their relations with Hanoi and Peking (and even with the United States) after American forces left the war and the Saigon and Phnom Penh regimes collapsed.

As regards China, Rusk was at pains to make it clear to everyone concerned--the Chinese leaders as well as the American people and Congress--that our involvement in Vietnam did not threaten Peking's interests. The growing Sino-Soviet conflict undoubtedly helped to divert the Chinese leaders' attention from the war in Indochina and the presence of U.S. forces near their southern border. Yet one of the greatest opportunities missed by the Johnson administration, because of its stubborn efforts in Vietnam, was the failure to take advantage of the Sino-Soviet split. Throughout the 1960s, this conflict was increasingly evident, but it was rarely even acknowledged by Rusk or Johnson.

In January 1968, communist forces launched attacks against every major city and town in South Vietnam. Despite their high casualties, they scored a major propaganda defeat against the Johnson administration. Americans began to realize that their government's only strategy was to hang on. Secretary Rusk favored a partial bombing halt, but Johnson was not yet willing to commit himself. (Rusk and a few other advisers knew by now that Johnson was not planning to run for reelection.)

On March 11 and 12, Secertary Rusk spent a total of eleven hours in the witness chair while the Senate Foreign Relations Committee questioned him about administration policy on live television. On March 12, Senator Eugene McCarthy, running as a peace candidate, received almost as many votes as President Johnson in the New Hampshire Democratic presidential primary. Rusk's position was made still more uncomfortable by press reports that General William Westmoreland had asked for 206,000 more troops. The New York Times said the request had "touched off a divisive internal debate within high levels of the Johnson Administration."

The Foreign Relations Committee had known for several days about the large troop request. But they did not know, and probably did not suspect, that Rusk and Johnson were considering announcing a partial bombing halt by the end of the month. The Committee wanted the Secretary to commit himself then and there to a deescalation of the war. Rusk politely declined to "speculate about decisions that have not been made and conclusions that have not been reached."

Outwardly, Rusk remained calm and dignified in the midst of the greatest public turmoil in a century of American history. Inwardly, he must have felt a profound sense of frustration. His anguish found expression in a rare public outburst to reporters on February 9, 1968, his fifty-ninth birthday. John Scali of ABC News asked if he was "satisfied" with American intelligence, which had failed to forecast the Tet offensive. "No," Rusk replied, "One is never satisfied

> But the point is I don't quite see why you have to start from the dissatisfaction. There gets to be a point when the question is whose side are you on. Now I'm Secretary of State of the United States, and I'm on our side. . . . On my fifty-ninth birthday forgive me if I express myself on these matters because none of your papers or your broadcasting apparatuses are worth a damn unless the United States succeeds. They are trivial compared to that question.[4]

On March 31, 1968, President Johnson announced to the country that he was cutting back the air war to the southern part of North Vietnam and that he would not seek re-election as President. He invited North Vietnam to engage in negotiations. Meanwhile, the ground war continued with limited U.S. reinforcements and heavy casualties on all sides.

Averell Harriman played the leading role in initial contacts with North Vietnamese officials. He and Cyrus Vance worked hard to get negotiations started before the November U.S. election. However, there was a tendency for all the parties involved (particularly Saigon) to wait and see who was elected to the White House and what position he would adopt.

Johnson and Rusk ended their final year in office with the country badly divided and their administration in disarray. Rusk was unfairly criticized in some quarters for not supporting Harriman's efforts to begin negotiations. There is every evidence that Rusk did support the negotiations and that he played a key role in persuading Johnson to reduce the bombing and then finally to end it.

FOOTNOTES

[1] See, for example, Foster Rhea Dulles, American Foreign Policy Toward Communist China, 1949-1969 (New York: T.Y. Crowell, 1972).

[2] P.A. Poole, Eight Presidents and Indochina (Huntington, N.Y.: Krieger, 1978), pp. 121-133.

[3] U.S. Senate, Committee on Foreign Relations, Hearings on Supplemental Appropriations, January 28, 1966.

[4] Quoted in Marvin Kalb and Elie Abel, Roots of Involvement (New York: Norton, 1971), p. 207.

Henry Kissinger

Chapter 7

KISSINGER AND INDOCHINA

When Nixon and Kissinger entered the White House, Indochina was a forest fire ranging out of control--well on its way to destroying our foreign policy consensus at home and our prestige abroad. During the next four years, Henry Kissinger devoted more of his time to Indochina than to any other subject. He gives it the same priority in his book, White House Years.

The passage of time and the new political climate have hardened Kissinger's views on Indochina (as on other key issues, such as SALT). He insists now that delaying our departure until the 1972 election--and camouflaging the retreat with sudden bursts of violence--provided a basis for negotiation. In retrospect, he admits to no qualms about the invasion of Cambodia. None of the awful consequences that seem to his critics to flow from that decision had any connection with the U.S. invasion, according to Dr. Kissinger. So far, no surprises.

Here and there, however, he adds a new twist that makes his account intriguing to the specialist as well as the general reader. For example, Spiro Agnew was the first member of the NSC to call for an attack on both Cambodian sanctuaries, the Fishhook and Parrot's Beak. Is Agnew being set up as a scapegoat? Quite the contrary, "Agnew was right," says Kissinger. History will reverse the shallow judgment of critics like William Shawcross and record how the administration's policies brought us "peace with honor." Congress is the real villain. It was they, the "opposition," who turned the hard-won victory into defeat.

So Kissinger has undertaken a formidable

assignment. With the aid of a dozen or more researchers, writers and editors, he seeks to describe one of the great man-made disasters of this century in a way that will enhance his own reputation and perhaps win him a second chance at high office. His chief asset, beyond the star quality which he still projects at Senate hearings, is a fund of amusing insider stories; these enliven a very long text and help to mask the completely fluid nature of his views.

Kissinger's ability to detach himself from past positions is truly formidable. We even find him "negotiating" with the Carter administration over the price of his political support for SALT II, his main objective during his last four years in office.

Kissinger has always described the Indochina issue to friends as his "nightmare." This was only partly because of the human suffering involved. War is not always hell; he plainly enjoyed his fast trips to Paris and his secret talks with Le Duc Tho. Yet each of their talks ended in frustration; Kissinger simply could not get a handle on the problem. The truly nightmarish feature of the war was the domestic conflict which it engendered. This, he knew, might undermine the stable world order which he was trying to create. Yet at times the administration's approach to the war seemed calculated to provoke Congress and divide the American people.

The central theme of Kissinger's thinking about Indochina was his belief that he could negotiate some kind of settlement with Hanoi. This view persisted throughout the next four years, even though, as he himself relates, the North Vietnamese were plainly under no pressure to come to terms. His other main theme was the notion, shared with many previous U.S. officials, that the country's and their own prestige had become involved in not losing the war.

Kissinger and Nixon have also been described by their critics as favoring a dramatic display of U.S. firepower--either to force Vietnam to give us better terms or simply to disguise our inability to match Hanoi's will.[1] This approach was first used against Cambodia and later in the mining of Haiphong and carpet-bombing of Hanoi. In his book, Kissinger claims to have supported each of these decisions on their merits. At the time, he often hinted to friends that he went along reluctantly and at least partly to preserve his influence on more important issues.[2] In White House Years, he sometimes paints himself as a super-hawk who favored the use of force more wholeheartedly than Nixon.

Kissinger developed a plan, in late 1969, which he called "Duck Hook." The idea was to make

> . . .the most sweeping and generous proposal of which we were capable, short of overthrowing an allied government but ensuring a free political contest. If it were refused, we would halt troop withdrawals and quarantine North Vietnam by mining its ports and perhaps bombing its rail links to China. The goal would be a rapid negotiated compromise.

Fortunately, this masterful scheme had to be abandoned because "there was not enough unanimity in our administration to pursue so daring and risky a course" (White House Years, pp. 284-85). Instead, the strategy of Vietnamization, favored by Secretary Laird, was chosen. The most likely reason Kissinger's "Duck Hook" plan was not adopted was that it made no political or military sense. It was guaranteed to produce deeper disunity at home, yet it was such an obvious bluff that it offered little hope of softening Hanoi's position. The Vietnamese leaders could see what was plain to all the world; complete U.S. withdrawal was only a matter of time.

Kissinger leaves unanswered the intriguing question of whether he thinks he or Nixon was the guiding force during their four years together before the Watergate scandal broke. Kissinger had, of course, made scathing personal comments about Nixon before being asked to join his staff. Once on board, it was only natural that he should study his new chief closely. There is no evidence that he shared Nixon's psychological need to assert a macho image. Yet Kissinger was astute enough to realize that Nixon was desperately in need of support and could not bear to be out-hawked by anyone in his immediate circle.

When the administration faced the first test of its mettle, the shooting down of a U.S. plane by North Korea, Kissinger describes how he longed to propose a punitive attack. Nixon backed off from the chllange, much to Kissinger's dismay. However, an opportunity to redeem this initial failure was not long in presenting itself.

Hanoi seemed to the Nixon administration to be testing them by violating an implied promise of military restraint. In response, the president began bombing suspected North Vietnamese sanctuaries in eastern Cambodia. Kissinger presents evidence that the younger liberals on his NSC staff shared his view that the bombing raids were necessary. As for himself, he argues that attacking a defenseless country had no moral significance because its neutrality had already been violated by North Vietnam. Moreover, he says that falsifying air force records of the bombing helped save Prince Sihanouk's face. This is true, though the real purpose was probably to prolong the administration's honeymoon with Congress. The net result of this weird combination of demonstrative force and secrecy was that no one took very much notice.

When the New York Times revealed the bombing in May 1969, Congress simply ignored it.

Evidently, the majority of members shared Senator Fulbright's optimism that Nixon had learned from Johnson's example and was looking for a way to end the war quickly. Congressional indifference to the bombing was reinforced when Prince Sihanouk told Senator Mansfield that he cared very little what was done as long as no Cambodians were killed. (There were 50,000 or so Montagnard tribesmen living in the provinces being bombed, but no one gave them much consideration.)

Kissinger recalls, in his book, that Hanoi never reacted to the secret bombing raids. There was no change in their conduct on the ground; nor did they alter their terms for ending the war. The secret bombing raids apparently made little difference to either side, psychologically or militarily.[3]

What was more important about the bombing was the fact that press leaks brought out Nixon's paranoia in the first months of his presidency. Moreover, his unhealthy reaction was evidently shared by his national security advisor. As Kissinger points out in his book, he was far from enjoying Nixon's full confidence at this stage. While Nixon bugged the oval office, Kissinger took care to record all his own phone conversations. (Shawcross quotes one which he received from a drunken Nixon and Bebe Rebozo while he was working on the invasion plan for Cambodia. Rebozo told Kissinger, on behalf of Nixon, that he would be fired if the invasion failed.)

Kissinger notes on several occasions that Nixon belittled the prospects for a negotiated settlement with Hanoi. Nevertheless, Kissinger stubbornly sought a mandate to try, and eventually he received it. What followed was predictable, even Kissinger concedes. Hanoi's representatives laughed politely at his jokes, but they refused to talk of anything but complete victory for their side. All Kissiner could do was gradually reduce his conditions for a truce. His only real leverage was that U.S. forces would eventually be out of Indochina, and then Hanoi would have to deal directly with Saigon.

From the U.S. standpoint, a great virtue of Vietnamization was that it did not need to be ratified by Hanoi. In theory, we could simply leave whenever the time seemed right. However, years of patron-client ties had conditioned everyone to expect South Vietnam to collapse as soon as our troops were out. What Thieu's government needed more than anything else was a breathing spell to consolidate its position. The perfect answer seemed to be to move the war westward into Cambodia. This is precisely what was done, though the idea does not seem to have occurred to anyone in Washington until March 1970, after Lon Nol ousted Prince Sihanouk.

As noted, Kissinger defends his role in the invasion of Cambodia by claiming it was a great military victory that saved many lives (as the bombing raids are also said to have done.) Moreover, he claims it was essential to keep Cambodia out of communist hands. The writing is much smoother than Nixon's "pitiful helpless giant" speech, but the logic is no less twisted. It is sometimes hard to know what represents honest confusion in Kissinger's mind and what is carefully contrived double-talk.

For example, if it was so important to prevent Cambodia from falling under communist control, the worst thing we could possibly have done was drive the North Vietnamese divisions deeper into the country. Worse still, we provided them with an imperative need to arm and train the Khmer Rouge, a previously insignficant element. By destroying the weak buffer state that had long separated Vietnam and Thailand, we jeopardized the security of the Thais, who have always been far better friends of the United States.

In short, by expanding the war into Cambodia, Nixon widened Hanoi's options and reduced his own.

As Secretary Rogers predicted, public support for an orderly process of disengagement reached a new low. Nixon's enforced decision to limit the U.S. invasion in time and space guaranteed that the situation would be vastly worse on Saigon's western flank when U.S. forces left than it had been two months earlier. All of eastern Cambodia except the road to Saigon (controlled by ARVN) was soon in communist hands. And Hanoi could move the war back into South Vietnam whenever it chose. The major politico-military result of the invasion was not that it helped buy a "decent interval" for Saigon. The main result was to forge a temporary alliance of Khmer and Vietnamese communists that lasted until their respective victories.

Many factors combined to bring about the death of Cambodia. Lon Nol's harassment of the sanctuaries, his pogrom against Vietnamese residents of Cambodia, and the anti-Khmer sentiments of both Vietnamese armies all played a part. But any honest account must give a key place in the chain of cause and effect to the U.S. invasion and our subsequent use of Cambodia to take the heat off Saigon.

In April 1972, the war returned to South Vietnam. North Vietnam launched a major invasion across the demilitarized zone. This was supported by Vietnamese communist attacks elsewhere in the South. The timing of the invasion, between Nixon's visit to China and his scheduled summit in Moscow suggested that Hanoi might be nervous about a "sellout" by her allies and was trying to force them to reaffirm their support.

President Nixon reacted to the new situation by ordering massive B-52 raids over much of North Vietnam and by mining Haiphong harbor. At the same time, however, he publicly restated his terms for an Indochina settlement, leaving out his demand that North Vietnam withdraw from the South. This virtually guaranteed that Hanoi would quickly gain control of South Vietnam.

During the summit meeting, Kissinger asked the Soviets to convey a further concession to Hanoi; he said he and Nixon were now prepared to have a tripartile commission composed of the Viet Cong, neutralists, and Saigon supporters supervise elections for a new national government in the South. The Soviets were reportedly stunned by this second major U.S. concession within a few weeks. However, Kissinger was jubilant when the Soviet leaders agreed to convey his message. He proudly informed one of his aides at the Moscow summit that the Russians "are going to help us."[4]

Within rather narrow limits, he may have been right. The Soviets may have tried to help the United States gain terms that would assist Nixon's chances of reelection. (Moscow had much more important matters than Indochina to discuss with Nixon and Kissinger.) The Soviets certainly could not afford to sell out their Vietnamese allies, as they did in 1954. But after Nixon made his key concessions, Brezhnev could urge Hanoi to allow the United States a "decent interval" in which to withdraw before completing the conquest of South Vietnam.

After several months of hard but inconclusive fighting between North and South Vietnamese forces, Hanoi apparently decided the time was ripe to end U.S. involvement in the war. On October 8, 1972, their negotiator, Le Duc Tho, tabled a draft agreement which he said would make it possible to reach agreement before the U.S. election.

The North Vietnamese draft called for an immediate cease-fire in place in South Vietnam, complete withdrawal of U.S. forces, and the return of our prisoners of war within sixty days. Vietnam was proclaimed to be one country, temporarily divided. But the most important feature of the draft was what it did not say. There was no requirement for a change of government in the South prior to the cease-fire.

Kissinger responded to this overture by conceding that Thieu's regime was not the sole legitimate administration in South Vietnam. This opened the way for settling lesser issues that mainly concerned the United States and North Vietnam. In a few days of intensive bargaining, Kissinger and Le Duc Tho reached a broad agreement, and some of its terms were published by Hanoi in late October. However, President Thieu in Saigon flatly refused to accept the agreement, and Nixon insisted on one more round of meetings to try to deal with some of Thieu's objections.

According to press reports, Kissinger began the session by placing the United States' maximum demands on the table, in effect withdrawing concessions he had made a month earlier. (He told some friends that he hoped it was clear to Le Duc Tho that he was doing this "for the record," i.e., to prove to Thieu that no better agreement could be obtained.) Kissinger may have hinted to Tho that the U.S. government would settle for minor "clarifications" of the October agreement.[5]

However, the North Vietnamese were obviously disturbed by Kissinger's presentation. They responded by saying they were no longer willing to release American prisoners of war in return for the withdrawal of all U.S. forces--unless Saigon set free the tens of thousands of civilian political prisoners it was holding. (This was a major aim of the Viet Cong.) Le Duc Tho also appears to have sought the right for Hanoi to move its troops back and forth freely across the line between North and South Vietnam.

While adopting this tough stand in the private November talks, Hanoi continued to demand publicly that the United States sign the October agreement as it stood. This, in effect, told Washington that Hanoi was prepared to forget (or reduce) its new demands if the United States did likewise.

Nixon ordered Kissinger to break off the talks. Returning to Washington, Kissinger told a press conference that Hanoi had reopened major points on which agreement had been reached, and that Nixon had therefore ordered a resumption of heavy bombing of North Vietnam.

No further explanation was offered by the Nixon administration for its decision. The president responded to the public's widespread dismay, confusion, and angry criticism of the "Christmas bombing" raids with icy silence. He had has landslide election behind him, and Congress was in recess and unlikely to take any firm countermeasures until February at the earliest. Nixon may have concluded that he was free to exert maximum pressure on North Vietnam for one brief final period. Even if this failed to change the terms of the peace agreement, no one would be able to say that he had allowed Congress or public opinion to prevent him from using American military power as he saw fit.

Leaders of both parties in Congress and of most governments that are normally friendly to the United States called for an end to the carpet bombing of North Vietnamese cities which, according to all reports, was far more indiscriminate and destructive of civilian life than any previous phase of the air war. Throughout December, Washington and Hanoi remained in contact, and when Nixon decided that he had made his point, he ordered the bombing cut back to the twentieth parallel. On January 8, 1973, Kissinger and Le Duc Tho resumed their talks. The resulting differences between the October and January versions of the agreement were minor and make Nixon's action seem all the more bizarre.

Congress quickly gave its approval to the Paris agreement, because it provided for the removal of our ground forces and the return of the POWs. However, this also removed the main constraint on Congress. From the start of Nixon's second term in 1973, he and Kissinger were forced by congressional pressures to defend--and then alter--important features of their foreign policy. The frontal assault by Congress gained strength as the Watergate scandal confirmed the view of many Americans that it had become almost routine for presidents to abuse their powers for purely political ends.

By early 1973, detente with Russia was beginning to turn sour. The first big sale of American grain had produced sharply rising food prices in America. Coupled with other factors, such as deficit funding of the Indochina war, the United States found itself with a massive problem of inflation. Our relations with Peking had also reached a plateau, because neither side was willing to budge on the Taiwan question. The Paris agreement which removed all U.S. troops and prisoners from Indochina, made it possible at last for Congress to mount a full-scale effort to limit the president's war powers. The first step was to pass the Church-Case resolution, which ended the air war in Indochina effective August 15, 1973.

Meanwhile, in March, the Washington Post broke the news of Watergate. President Nixon tried to strengthen his suddenly frail administration by nominating Kissinger as secretary of state. During 1973 and 1974, Kissinger seemed reluctant to have anything to do with Indochina. He plainly hoped this nightmare would not come back to haunt him. On several occasions, he publicly criticized North Vietnamese violations of the Paris agreement; he had little to say about Saigon's conduct, though he plainly despised President Thieu.

Though the Paris agreement ended direct U.S. involvement in the war, it brought neither peace nor a political settlement to Indochina. Congress had no intention of allowing U.S. forces to return to the quagmire, and thus began to place new restrictions on American aid to Vietnam and the way in which it was administered.

Each new control tended to place the leaders of South Vietnam and Cambodia in a more delicate position. They had to decide whether to gamble their limited stocks of fuel and ammunition on a crash effort to improve their position. If they took this chance, they knew Congress might not resupply them--even if their military gamble succeeded. Would it be safer, therefore, to hoard their materiel and hope that time might somehow prove to be on their side?

In April 1974, Thieu decided to gamble. ARVN forces managed to trap most of North Vietnam's Seventh Division in the Parrot's Beak area of eastern Cambodia. The victory seemed solid; Hanoi even failed to exploit its opportunity to attack the northern provinces.

But Saigon had drawn heavily on its reserves of fuel and ammunition. At President Thieu's request, the American mission ordered replacement stocks, in May 1974, which were designed to prepare Saigon for an expected North Vietnamese offensive. Since funds for the fiscal year had been used up (partly by rising costs of crude oil), the new orders were to be paid for out of next year's funds.

Ambassador Graham Martin had imposed a ban on official reporting of the ARVN operation in Cambodia. Thus, both Congress and the executive branch first learned of it from the Washington Post, which condemned it as a violation of the Paris agreement. In Congress, Senator Kennedy gained swift approval for an amendment which denied the supplemental funding--and ended the practice of paying for aid shipments with funds that had not yet been appropriated.

A few months later, Congress reduced fiscal 1975 aid to Vietnam to $700 million, half of the Nixon administration's request. Similar cuts

were made for Cambodia. Congress also required
the creation of a single, highly visible account
for military aid to Vietnam, which was subject
to periodic audit. These actions signaled to
Vietnamese and Cambodian leaders that the end
of U.S. aid was in sight. One effect was to
weaken military morale very sharply.

With these events as prelude, it was hardly
surprising that Congress reacted negatively in
late 1974, when President Ford requested supplemental aid for Vietnam and Cambodia. Some of
the intense suspicion which members of Congress
and their staff had previously directed at
Nixon was now focused on Secretary Kissinger.

Both Congress and the White House recognized,
in the winter of 1974-75, that it was doubtful
whether Saigon or Phnom Penh could survive
another dry season campaign--which might continue as late as July 1975. The basic rationale
offered by Kissinger for supplementary aid was
that the people of Saigon and Phnom Penh deserved
the right to choose whether to fight or surrender.
Refusing to provide supplementary aid would
deny them that right because it would leave them
almost no reserves of ammunition and fuel.

During February and early March 1975, a
group of congressmen visited South Vietnam and
Cambodia. They saw that the situation was
crumbling rapidly as a result of incompetent
leadership in both countries. Their report,
when they returned to Washington, strongly
influenced their colleagues. Congress was moving
toward the position that it would be more humane
to end the war by withholding arms aid than to
allow the killing to go on. Many congressmen also
feared that the administration was moving far too
slowly in the evacuation of thousands of Americans
who remained in Vietnam. About 2000 were
evacuated during February and March, but 4000
remained in mid-April.

Meanwhile, the collapse of resistance by the Cambodian government followed inevitably after Khmer Communists gained control of the Mekong River in January 1975. Communist forces were on the outskirts of the capital by early April, and they took control of Phnom Penh on April 17. The evacuation of all American nationals and 194 local employees was orderly, in contrast to the situation in Vietnam.

The crumbling of South Vietnam's resistance followed a similar timetable. During the last hectic days that remained, between the surrender of Phnom Penh and the fall of Saigon, Kissinger and Congress engaged in an unedifying duel, each trying to place the blame on the other.

Thus began Kissinger's worst year in office. Although, oddly, he continued to enjoy great personal esteem on Capitol Hill, every one of his key positions was sharply questioned--detente, step-by-step diplomacy in the Middle East, the danger of Eurocommunism, aid to Turkey, the heavy transfer of arms to the Third World, and finally the secret war in Angola. 1975 ended with a stunning congressional veto of Kissinger's policy in southern Africa. President Ford relieved him of his post as national security advisor and banned the word "detente" from his vocabulary. Although Kissinger revived his public image by reversing his African policy, President Ford lost the 1976 election by a small margin.

FOOTNOTES

[1] Tad Szulc, The Illusion of Peace, New York: Viking, 1978, pp. 36-39 and ff. See also William Shawcross, Sideshow, New York: Simon and Schuster, 1979, pp. 128-149.

[2] One can also find a transitional image, based on 1975 or 1976 interviews with his friend, John Stoessinger, in Stoessinger's Henry Kissinger: The Anguish of Power, New York: Norton, 1976, pp. 49-77.

[3] Kissinger cites Prince Sihanouk's remark, in April 1979, that the North Vietnamese "were not impressed" by the bombing.

[4] Szulc, op.cit., pp. 572-73.

[5] See Flora Lewis, "How Compromise Was Reached," New York Times, January 25, 1973. In addition to supporting Thieu's objections, Kissinger also probably tried to clarify the supervisory procedures for the truce and to have the English text of the agreement given the same official status as the Vietnamese text.

Cyrus Vance

Chapter 8

CYRUS VANCE: FOCUS ON THE THIRD WORLD

During the Johnson years, Cyrus Vance won respect as a skilled, behind-the-scenes negotiator. A corporation lawyer by training, his final task for Johnson was to help Averell Harriman get the Paris peace talks started during 1968. In 1977, he assumed the extremely difficult role of translating President Carter's foreign affairs goals into reality.

Many of the Carter administration's initial foreign policy objectives--such as support for human rights, disengagement from Korea, and recognition of Hanoi--had been espoused for many years by Congressional liberals. Jimmy Carter adopted these views during the 1976 campaign, and Vance appointed a number of Congressional staffers who had served in the Carter campaign to key positions in the State Department.

As Secretary of State, Vance worked more closely with the Department than many of his predecessors, notably Henry Kissinger, had done. During three years in office, he mainly emphasized the need for better relations with the Third World, and much progress was made in this area. Vance and others in the administration helped the British government resolve the long-standing problem of Zimbabwe. Working with our major allies, Vance also made headway on disentangling the status of Namibia. The Panama Canal Treaty removed another serious irritant in our relations with the southern hemisphere.

Recognition of China was accomplished without abandoning Taiwan. There was even a net gain in confidence on the part of our other Asian allies, because the Carter administration wisely shelved its plan to pull U.S. troops out of Korea. In the Middle East, the Camp David accords gave momentum to the search for Middle Eastern peace. Of course, none of these efforts received praise in all quarters. Their importance can only be judged after the dust of current crises has begun to settle.

Vance failed to persuade the Senate to ratify SALT II, though he was not alone in being responsible for this failure. The episode illustrates clearly the fact that he was not the kind of statesman who seeks to shape the climate of public opinion while in office. He seemed to have little eloquence. While a diplomat is probably wise to sacrifice drama for precision in his public statements, Vance was unusually bland in public. No doubt he gave his main time and energy to those aspects of the job in which he knew he could be most effective.

Though the task of being chief administration lobbyist for foreign policy comes with the portfolio, a Secretary can choose whether to budget time on seeking support from public interest groups or to deal directly with Congress. Vance chose the latter course. At first, Kissinger proved to be a very hard act for him to follow, but Vance came to be regarded as an effective advocate.

Though he probably had little taste for political jockeying, Vance also had to compete for recognition as the president's senior foreign policy advisor against such seasoned operators as national security advisor Zbigniew Brzezinski and Defense Secretary Harold Brown. Even the U.S. Ambassador to the United Nations, Andrew Young, sometimes gave the impression of making U.S. policy on his own. Only by resigning, ostensibly because he was overruled on the Iranian rescue mission, did Vance finally manage to make leading elements of American society more aware of the erosion of the secretary of state's position.

Shortly after leaving office, Vance gave the Commencement address at Harvard. This speech attracted widespread interest as a clear and eloquent statement of the position that North-South relations deserve as much attention as relations with our allies and with the Soviet Union. Vance said we must maintain the nuclear balance with Russia. But he strongly implied that the old hierarchy of issues--in which East-West relations came before all else (and might thus be thought to permeate all other issues)--was no longer valid.

This lack of hierarachy is one of the main tenets of the modernist school of international relations--as distinct from the realist or traditionalist school, of which Kissinger and Brzezinski are leading exponents. (Besides Vance, two major figures associated with Harvard, Stanley Hoffmann and Joseph Nye, are important spokesmen of the modernist view-point.) The reason Cyrus Vance's speech attracted so much attention may be that Americans are hungry for serious debate and reasoned discussion about the direction U.S. policy should take in the final years of what has been called the "American Century."

Address by Former Secretary of State Cyrus Vance
Harvard Commencement Exercises, June 5, 1980

Yours is the first Harvard class to graduate in the decade of the 1980's. The decisions our nation makes now will shape the future of that decade.

We can either work to shape, in a wise and effective manner, the changes that now engulf our world or, by acting unwisely, become shackled by them.

It is time to set and stick to basic goals. Neither we nor the world can afford an American foreign policy which is hostage to the emotions of the moment.

We must have in our minds a conception of the world we want a decade hence. The 1990 we seek must shape our actions in 1980, or the decisions of 1980 could give us a 1990 we will regret.

Basic Goals Are Defined

Supporting the efforts of third world nations to preserve their independence and to improve the quality of life for their people, particularly those hovering at the edge of survival; strengthening the health and well-being of our economic system within a strong international economy.

These are the decisions, along with preserving the military balance while effectively managing our competition with the Soviet Union and fostering strong alliances of free nations-- these are the decisions we should make now.

These goals are ambitious. It would be naive to think otherwise. But unless our reach is bold, our grasp will fall far short.

Let us keep in mind the world from which we start: a world undergoing rapid change, with growing expectations, better education, quickened communications; a world in which neither the United States nor any other country commands a preponderance of power or a monopoly of wisdom. It is a world of conflicts, among nations and values, among social systems and emerging new interests. It is a world in which competitive superpowers hold in their hands our common survival, yet paradoxically find it beyond their power to order events.

Rejecting the Gloomy Outlook

There is a disturbing fear in the land that we are no longer capable of shaping our future. Some believe that we have lost our military muscle; others worry that our political will has been sapped.

I do not accept this gloom. It discards the abiding pragmatic philosophy that has characterized America ever since its founding.

I consider mistaken the view that we and we alone are responsible for all the confusing changes that we see around us. This is a serious misreading of our condition, a perverted hubris that over-estimates our power and our responsibility for ill and underestimates our capacity for good.

The international diffusion of power and intellect is a fact. It will not change. It requires fresh and vital forms of action, not regret and pining for supposed "good old days."

What is to be regretted is a reluctance to relate our basic purposes to these new conditions. Yesterday's answers will not provide tomorrow's solutions.

It seems to me that much of the current dissatisfaction with the world and our role in it rests on certain fallacies. These illusions must be exploded before our nation can chart a coherent and determined course in foreign policy.

The first fallacy is that a single strategy-- a master plan--will yield the answers to each and every foreign policy decision we face. Whatever value that approach may have had in a bipolar world, it now serves us badly. The world has become pluralistic, exposing the inadequacy of the single strategy, the grand design, where facts are forced to fit theory. Given the complexity of the world to which we have fallen heir, the effect of a single strategy is to blur this complexity and to divide nations everywhere into friends and enemies.

Fear of Getting Second Best

A second widely accepted fallacy is the fear of negotiation, the worry that somehow we will always come out second best in any bargain. This fallacy assumes we have a realistic alternative of going it alone, of not bothering to recognize the legitimate interests and desires of other peoples. Without the fair bargain, achieved through negotiation and diplomacy, there is only a misguided, failed effort to impose one will upon another.

Denying others a fair bargain and its benefits will not alter their behavior or reduce their power; it will simply have the effect of denying ourselves the same advantages. If America fears to negotiate with our adversaries, or to bargain fairly with third world nations, we will not have a diplomacy. And we, no less than others, will be the loser.

A third myth that needs to be exploded is that there is an incompatibility between the pursuit of America's values in our foreign policy, such as human rights, and the pursuit of our interests.

Certainly the pursuit of human rights must be managed in a practical way. We must constantly weigh how best to encourage progress while maintaining an ability to conduct business with governments--even unpopular ones--in countries where we have important security interests.

Choice: Freedom or Convulsion

But we must ultimately recognize that the demand for individual freedom and economic progress cannot be long repressed without sowing the seeds of violent convulsion. Thus it is in our interest to support constructive change, as we did, for example, in the Dominican Republic, and are seeking to do in Central America, before the alternatives of radicalism or repression force out moderate solutions.

We know from our own national experience that the drive for human freedom has tremendous force and vitality. It is universal. It is resilient. And, ultimately, it is irrepressible.

In a profound sense, then, our ideals and our interests coincide. For we have a stake in the stability that comes when people can express their hopes and build their futures freely.

Further is the dangerous fallacy of the military solution to nonmilitary problems. It arises in particularly acute form at times of frustration, when the processes of negotiations are seen as slow-moving and tedious.

American military power is essential to maintaining the global military balance. Our defense forces must be modernized--and they will be. But increased military power is a basis, not a substitute, for diplomacy.

I have heard it argued that our response to a changing world must be a new emphasis on American military power and the will to use it. This is reflected in proposed new budget priorities in the Congress, in which unnecessary defense spending squeezes out domestic programs and foreign assistance. There is near-consensus on the need for defense increases. But it is illusion to believe that they are a substitute for the diplomacy and resources needed to address such problems as internal change and basic need in other nations or a battered international economy.

The Right to Shape the Future

The use of military force is not, and should not be, a desirable American policy response to the internal politics of other nations. We believe we have the right to shape our future; we must respect that right in others. We must clearly understand the distinction between our readiness to act forcefully when the vital interests of our nation, our allies and our friends are threatened, and our recognition that our military force cannot provide a satisfactory answer to the purely internal problems of other nations.

Finally there is a pervasive fallacy that America could have the power to order the world just the way we want it to be. It assumes, for example, that we could dominate the Soviet Union--that we could prevent it from being a superpower--if we chose to do so. This obsolete idea has more to do with nostalgia than with present-day reality.

Spread over the widest territory of any nation on earth, the Soviet Union has its own strategic interests and goals. From a state of underdevelopment and the ravages of war, it has built formidable military and industrial resources. We should not underestimate these resources any more than we should exaggerate them. We must preserve and manage a position of essential equivalence with the Soviet Union. It is naive to believe that the Russians will play by our rules any more than we will accept theirs. It is naive to believe that they--any more than we--would willingly accept a position of second best in military strength.

A dangerous new nostalgia underlies all these fallacies--a longing for earlier days when the world seemed, at least in retrospect, to have been a more orderly place in which American power could, alone, preserve that order. That nostalgia continually erodes confidence in our national leadership for it encourages expectations that bear no relationship to reality. And it makes change in the world's condition seem all threat and no opportunity. It makes an unruly world seem more hostile than it is. The fact is that we are a people who not only have adapted well to change but have thrived on it.

'Self-Indulgent Nonsense'

The new nostalgia leads us to simplistic solutions and go-it-alone illusions, diverting our energies from the struggle to shape change in constructive directions. It is self-indulgent nonsense, bound to lead us into error, if not disaster.

What course is open to us now?

Our real problems are long term in nature. It will not do to reach for the dramatic act, to seek to cut through stubborn dilemmas with a single stroke. Against the real problems now facing us this approach will not only fall far short but also create new problems.

Obviously, immediate crises have to be dealt with as they occur. And we should learn from these events. But they should never be allowed to distort our foreign-policy goals.

As a global power the United States has an extraordinary range of interests. This is why we must make sure that our pursuit of the desirable does not interfere with our achievement of the essential.

If, by 1990, we have not made progress in the four basic areas I listed earlier, the world will indeed be the inhospitable place many now fear it is. In each area we can make progress--if. If we listen to our hopes no less than our fear. If we are prepared to sacrifice now for our future good. And, most important, if we work with other nations to resolve problems none can solve alone.

First, we must preserve the global military balance and achieve, as well, balance in our political relations with the Soviet Union.

Our military strength is important to our own safety, to a strong foreign policy free from coercion, to the confidence of allies and friends, and to the future of the reciprocal arms control and other negotiations. Our strength also buttresses regional balances that could be upset by the direct or indirect use of Soviet power.

Arms Control Termed Vital

Maintaining the military balance will be expensive. To limit the costs, and to increase our safety, we must have an effective arms-control policy as an integral part of our security policy.

Yet when the historian of 1990 looks back upon the year 1980, I believe a profound mistake may well be identified: a failure to ratify the SALT II treaty. As a symbol of our hopes for a more peaceful world, as a commitment to work toward better security through arms control and as a process of trying to work out differences with an adversary, this treaty stands at the very heart of a sensible and far-seeing American foreign policy.

Without this treaty our efforts to prevent the spread of nuclear weapons will be in jeopardy. If the United States and the Soviet Union fail to make real headway toward controlling nuclear weapons and eliminating nuclear teating, nonnuclear nations will have less reason for their own restraint.

Without this treaty both sides will have more nuclear weapons than with it. In particular, the Soviet Union will have thousands of additional nuclear warheads.

Without this treaty it will be much more difficult for us to undertake reliable planning for our military forces since we will not be in as good a position to know what is going on within the Soviet Union. The treaty bans practices that would prevent each side from being able to verify compliance with its terms.

Conflict or Cooperation

Without this treaty there is bound to be less emphasis placed in both of our societies on conciliation of differences without conflict. Political elements who wish to emphasize conflict over cooperation will be strengthened.

Without this treaty the process of arms control might be dealt a blow from which it could not recover. Can anyone doubt that this will make the coming decade more dangerous?

It is not too late, but it may soon be. I believe that the Senate must ratify the SALT II treaty before the end of this year. Certainly we must continue our firm and sustained response to Soviet aggression against Afghanistan. But neither that aggression nor the fact that this is a political year are sufficient grounds for a failure to act in our own national interests. I am aware of the political difficulties in acting at this time. But if we fail to act we will someday ask ourselves why we were blinded by considerations of the moment and lost a vital long-term opportunity. It is far too easy, in an election year, to let what may seem smart politics produce bad policies.

Both the United States and the Soviet Union will have to work even harder in the years ahead to avoid extremely serious confrontations. How we conduct our relations with the Soviet Union will perhaps be the most significant test of our maturity of judgment, our clearsighted recognition of real interests and our capacity for leadership.

From Deterrence to Incentives

It is foolish and dangerous to believe that we can manage this relationship by deterrence alone. We also will need to provide positive incentives.

We must use both our strength and the prospects of mutually beneficial agreements to help shape competition with the Soviet Union. We must work for implicit if not explicit agreements to bound our competition by restraints, by a kind of common law of competition.

The means to implement this goal will rest on patience, steadiness, clarity and consistency. In our approach toward Moscow we cannot afford wild swings from being too trusting to being hysterical. And even as we maintain a steady course we must recognize that it will require constant effort to mold that common law of competition. That effort must include both deterrence and the possibility of cooperation where our interests coincide.

We must also think anew about how to manage our affairs with the People's Republic of China in relation to those with the Soviet Union. Even as we act to develop nonmilitary ties with China we should strive to restore a more balanced approach to both countries.

Nurturing Strong Alliances

A second and paramount goal for our nation should be to nurture strong alliances among free nations.

But there is no gainsaying that relations among the industrial democracies are uneasy. We must address the causes for this; they may well be more fundamental in origin than we care to admit.

We must find better ways to coordinate our policies in areas beyond our territories, for it is there that we increasingly face new problems. While our immediate interests may sometimes diverge in such areas, our basic interests run in parallel and, accordingly, should provide grounds for common action.

Our allies must recognize that while the American nuclear shield is unshakeable and our commitment to the common defense is firm, they cannot expect America to bear a disproportionate share of the burdens of deterrence.

We, for our part, must accept the other side of the same coin. We need common efforts because we cannot bear all the burdens ourselves, nor do we have all the answers. The price to us will be a willingness to consult and adjust for the sake of allied agreement. Consultation cannot be a substitute for a clear sense of direction. But there is no point in consulting if we are unwilling then to adjust our course for the sake of a common purpose.

Potential Cockpit of Crisis

Partly because of the strength of our alliances, it is the third world--more than our alliance areas--that is likely to be the cockpit of crises in the coming decade.

We must first be clear on the nature of our challenge there.

Certainly, as we have seen in Afghanistan and elsewhere in the third world, Soviet actions pose threats we must meet.

But we will meet them ineffectually if we react only by immitating Soviet tactics--emphasizing the military at the expense of the political and disregarding the indigenous yearning of third world nations for true independence and economic justice.

We must recognize the strong sense of national pride--and fierce independence--of developing nations. Having fought to throw off the burden of outside domination, they will strenuously reject the efforts of other nations to impose their will. We should respect and reinforce that spirit of independence. Our interests are not served by their being like us but by their being free to join with us in meeting the goals we share.

Support for the political independence and economic growth of the poorer nations is important primarily because these nations matter in their own right. Their conflicts could also become our wars. Our trade with them is increasing. Their instabilities can affect our interests in many ways.

Our own national interests are served when we support the security of third world nations with our assistance. When we help them develop their economies, we not only meet pressing human needs, we invest in important trading relationships. Our interests are served by supporting peaceful change within those nations and by encouraging the peaceful resolution of their conflicts.

Absence of a Realistic Plan

For example, our interest are clearly served by our efforts to help resolve the Arab-Israeli conflict and bring peace to this troubled and vitally important region.

In 1990, as in 1980, the problems of the third world will remain a central challenge to our wisdom. No realistic plan yet exists to defuse the potential dangers or resolve all the anguish of hundreds of millions of people living in degrading poverty. But over the next decade the United States can make a difference with regard to the severity of those problems--in helping create progress and hope, in not disregarding the violence and suffering of despair.

To make that difference we must first accept our differences with third world nations, yet work with them where our interests coincide. Peace came to Zimbabwe because of the ability of Britain and the United States to work with the African nations of the region. Had the opponents of improved relations with Mozambique, Zambia, Tanzania and others had their way, the situation today might well have been far different. The logical corollary is clear; it makes no sense not to recognize the Government of Angola, a Government with which we have cooperated in the search for peace in southern Africa despite fundamental differences on other issues.

It is imperative that we also put our resources behind our policies.

American aid programs comprise less than 1.5 percent of our Federal budget. They--not rhetoric, not good will--are what make the most difference in supporting our third world diplomacy and in addressing now the causes of later crises. Yet they are under constant assault in the Congress and elsewhere.

'Disgraceful' Deficiency in Aid

The result is--I can think no other word--disgraceful.

Our security assistance has declined by 25 percent over the past 20 years.

The United States ranks 13th among the 17 major industrial powers in percentage of G.N.P. devoted to development assistance. We will likely soon drop another notch.

We are far in arrears in meeting the pledges we have made to the multilateral development banks--and likely to slip still farther.

It is not enough to strengthen our defenses. We must also increase the resources needed to support our diplomacy, a diplomacy designed to reduce the chances our military forces may be needed.

Other nations do not want the rhetoric of American leadership; they want its substance. And we must provide it. The U.N. global negotiations on relations between developed and developing countries--opening this fall in New York--offers a prime opportunity for us to demonstrate that leadership.

This bring me to a fourth goal for the decade: a strong American economy in a strong international economy.

I ask you to ponder the implications for our future of two stark statistics:

According to the International Energy Agency, based on current trends, by 1985 world demand for oil is likely to outstrip global oil production by two million barrels a day. Consider the implications of this fact for world oil prices, and our own economy; for the hard pressed economies of the poorer nations; for relations among the industrial nations, if there is a new scramble for energy.

Domestic Productivity Decline

The other statistic is domestic in nature: Productivity in the United States declined in every quarter of 1979 after the rate of increase in our productivity had steadily slowed over the previous two decades. Decreasing productivity not only fuels inflation. It undercuts our trading position and the strength of the dollar. And declining productivity means increasing domestic pressures for protectionism.

In both cases--meeting the energy crisis and addressing the problem of productivity--we cannot rely on the genius of some economist with a new solution. We need acts of political will.

If the U.S. and the other industrial countries do not act decisively to reduce our levels of energy consumption, and particularly our demand for oil, we will stand on the brink of economic disaster by the end of the decade--or sooner. The effort must be made now.

The President recognized the danger posed by our energy dependence and, from the earliest days of the Administration, sought comprehensive legislation to deal with it. Public skepticism and Congressional inaction have delayed the full implementation of his program for three costly years. In the meantime the oil exporters have added price increase after price increase at will and used their oil power for political ends. This will not change unless we are willing to let domestic energy prices reflect the reality of the marketplace and to tax excessive use ourselves instead of letting OPEC do it for us; unless we produce more energy-efficient cars and houses and appliances and channel sufficient resources into developing alternative energy sources; unless we share equitably with other industrial countries the burden of conservation and stand together against unjustifiable price increases.

A Question of National Will

U.S. productivity declined in every quarter last year. Solving that problem will also be costly. But there must be reduced consumption and a higher rate of capital investment; a willingness to shift from obsolete industries instead of propping them up with protectionist trade barriers; incentives for innovation; responsible price and wage demands by industry and labor. Each is at root a question not of economic theory but of national will.

Meeting the four challenges I have described depends not on quick fixes, new gimmicks, bluffs or threats. It requires steadiness, political will, and understanding of a world in change.

If we are prepared to accept the implications of a world of diffuse power, and work with others where we cannot succeed alone, there need be no insurmountable barriers to our progress.

There should be no mystery about how to manage East-West relations with realism and prudence, creating more cooperative alliances, addressing the problems of third world nations and acting now to strengthen our economy for later.

The mystery will be for the historian of 1990, if--blinded by the new nostalgia--we fail now to shape our future. The puzzle will be why we reacted against change in the world and did not seek to shape it. The historian will then conclude that ours was a failure not of opportunity but of seeing opportunity; a failure not of resources but of the wisdom to use them; a failure not of intellect but of understanding and of will.

It need not be so. For now, as always before, our destiny is in our hands.

SUGGESTIONS FOR READING

    I. Memoirs and Biographies
   II. Executive Branch Leadership
  III. The Second World War
  IV. The Cold War and U.S.-Soviet Relations
   V. Bureaucracy and Foreign Policy
  VI. National Security Policy
 VII. The Politics of Foreign Policy
VIII. U.S. Policy Toward East Asia
  IX. The Indochina War
   X. U.S. Foreign Economic Policy
  XI. Surveys of U.S. Foreign Relations

* * * *

I. Memoirs and Biographies

Acheson, Dean. Present at the Creation: My Years at the State Department. New York: Norton, 1969.

Bohlen, Charles E. Witness to History, 1939-1969. New York: Norton, 1973.

Clay, Lucius D. Decision in Germany. Garden City, N.Y.: Doubleday, 1950.

Dobney, Frederick J. (editor). Selected Papers of Will Clayton. Baltimore: Johns Hopkins Press, 1971.

Eden, Anthony. Full Circle. Boston: Houghton Mifflin, 1960.

Eisenhower, Dwight D. The White House Years. 2 vols. Garden City, N.Y.: Doubleday, 1963.

Eisenhower, Milton S. The President Is Calling. Garden City, N.Y.: Doubleday, 1974.

Emmerson, John K. The Japanese Thread: A Life in the U.S. Foreign Service. New York: Holt, Rinehart and Winston, 1978.

Ferrell, Robert H. American Diplomacy in the Great Depression: Hoover-Stimson Foreign Policy, 1929-1933. New Haven Conn.: Yale University Press, 1957.

_____. George C. Marshall. New York: Cooper Square, 1966.

Finer, Herman. Dulles over Suez: The Theory and Practice of His Diplomacy. Chicago: Quadrangle, 1964.

Gerson, Louis L. John Foster Dulles. New York: Cooper Square, 1967.

Graubrad, Stephen R. Kissinger: Portrait of a Mind. New York: Norton, 1973.

Harriman, W. Averell and Elie Abel. Special Envoy to Churchill and Stalin, 1941-1946. New York: Random House, 1975.

Herz, Martin F. (ed.). Decline of the West? George Kennan and His Critics. Washington, D.C. Ethics and Public Policy Center, Georgetown University, 1978.

Hilsman, Roger. To Move a Nation: The Politics of Policy-Making in the Administration of John F. Kennedy. Garden City, N.Y.: Doubleday, 1967

Hoopes, Townsend. The Devil and John Foster Dulles. Boston: Little, Brown, 1973.

Kennan, George F. Memoirs. Vol. 1, 1925-1950. Vol. 2, 1950-1963. Boston: Atlantic Monthly Press, 1967, 1972.

Kissinger, Henry. The White House Years. Boston: Little, Brown, 1979.

Lyon, Peter. *Eisenhower: Portrait of the Hero.* Boston: Little, Brown, 1974.

Paper, Lewis J. *The Promise and the Performance: The Leadership of John F. Kennedy.* New York: Crown, 1975.

Pratt, Julius W. *Cordell Hull.* 2 Vols. New York: Cooper Square, 1964.

Rappaport, Armin. *Henry L. Stimson and Japan.* Chicago: University of Chicago Press, 1963.

Schlesinger, Arthur M., Jr. *A Thousand Days: John F. Kennedy in the White House.* Boston: Houghton, Mifflin, 1965.

Smith, Gaddis. *Dean Acheson.* New York: Cooper Square, 1972.

Sorenson, Theodore C. *Kennedy.* New York: Harper and Row, 1965.

Stimson, Henry L., and McGeorge Bundy. *On Active Service in Peace and War.* New York: Harper and Row, 1948.

Stoessinger, John. *The Anguish of Power.* New York: Norton, 1976.

Szulc, Tad. *The Illusion of Peace: Foreign Policy in the Nixon Years.* New York: Viking, 1978.

Truman, Harry S. *Years of Trial and Hope.* Garden City, New York: Doubleday, 1955-56.

White, Theodore H. *In Search of History.* New York: Harper and Row, 1978.

Williams, William Appleman. *Some Presidents: Wilson to Nixon.* New York: The New York Review, 1972.

II. Executive Branch Leadership

Bernstein, Carl, and Bob Woodward. All the President's Men. New York: Simon and Schuster, 1974.

Berger, Raoul. Executive Privilege: A Constitutional Myth. Cambridge, Mass.: Harvard University Press, 1974.

Burns, James MacGregor. Leadership. New York: Harper, 1978.

Donovan, John C. The Cold Warriors: A Policy-Making Elite. Lexington, Mass.: Heath, 1974.

Fulbright, J. William. The Cripplied Giant: American Foreign Policy and Its Domestic Consequences. New York: Random House, 1972.

Graebner, Norman A. (ed.). An Uncertain Tradition: American Secretaries of State in the Twentieth Century. New York: McGraw-Hill, 1961.

Halberstam, David. The Best and Brightest. New York: Random House: 1972.

III. The Second World War

Churchill, Winston S. The Second World War. 6 vols. Boston: Houghton, Mifflin, 1948-53.

Myer, Dillon S. Uprooted Americans. Tuscon: University of Arizona Press, 1971.

Smith, Gaddis. American Diplomacy and the Second World War. New York: Wiley, 1965.

IV. The Cold War and U.S.-Soviet Relations

Alperovitz, Gar. Cold War Essays. Garden City: N.Y.: Anchor Books, 1970.

Backer, John H. The Decision to Divide Germany. Durham, N.C.: Duke University Press, 1978.

Davis, Lynn Etheridge. The Cold War Begins: Soviet-American Conflict Over Eastern Europe. Princeton: Princeton University Press, 1974.

Etzold, Thomas H., and John Lewis Gaddis, (eds.). Containment: Documents on American Policy and Strategy. New York: Columbia University Press, 1978.

Gaddis, John Lewis. Russia, the Soviet Union, and the United States: An Interpretive History. New York: Wiley, 1978.

──────. The United States and the Origins of the Cold War, 1941-1947. New York: Columbia University Press, 1972.

Gardner, Lloyd C. Architects of Illusion: Men and Ideas in American Foreign Policy, 1941-1949. Chicago: Quadrangle, 1970.

Kennan, George F. Russia and the West Under Lenin and Stalin. Boston: Little, Brown, 1960.

Khrushchev, N.S. Khrushchev Remembers. Boston: Little, Brown, 1974.

Ulam, Adam B. The Rivals: America and Russia Since World War II. New York: Viking, 1971.

V. Bureaucracu and Foreign Policy

Bacchus, William I. Foreign Policy and the Bureaucratic Process: The State Department's Country Director System. Princeton: Princeton University Press, 1974.

Destler, I.M. Presidents, Bureaucrats, and Foreign Policy. Princeton: Princeton University Press, 1972.

Franck, Thomas M., and Edward Weisband (eds.). *Secrecy and Foreign Policy*. New York: Oxford University Press, 1974.

Marchetti, Victor and John D. Marks. *The CIA and the Cult of Intelligence*. New York: Knopf, 1974.

Rusk, Dean. *The Craft of Diplomacy*. New York: Praeger, 1967.

Schulzinger, Robert D. *The Making of the Diplomatic Mind: The Training, Outlook and Style of United States Foreign Service Officers, 1908-1931*. Middletown, Conn.: Wesleyan University Press, 1975.

Weil, Martin. *A Pretty Good Club: The Founding Fathers of the U.S. Foreign Service*. New York: Norton, 1978.

Werking, Richard Hume. *The Master Architects: Building the United States Foreign Service, 1899-1913*. Lexington, Ky.: University Press of Kentucky, 1977.

VI. National Security Policy and Policy-Making

Allison, Graham. *Essence of Decision: Explaining the Cuban Missile Crisis*. Boston: Little, Brown, 1971.

Bell, Coral. *The Diplomacy of Detente: The Kissinger Era*. New York: St. Martin's, 1977.

Bobrow, D.E. (ed.). *Weapons System Decisions*. New York: Praeger, 1969.

Boulding, Kenneth E. *Conflict and Defense: A General Theory*. New York: Harper and Row, 1968.

Dougherty, J.E. How to Think About Arms Control and Disarmament. New York: Crane, Russak, 1973.

Feit, Edward. The Armed Bureaucrats. Boston: Houghton, Mifflin, 1973.

George, Alexander L., and Richard Smoke. Deterrence in American Foreign Policy: Theory and Practice. New York: Columbia University Press, 1974.

Kennedy, Robert F. Thirteen Days: A Memoir of the Cuban Missile Crisis. New York: Norton, 1969.

Kissinger, Henry A. Nuclear Weapons and Foreign Policy.

Schelling, Thomas C. The Strategy of Conflict. Cambridge, Mass.: Harvard University Press, 1960.

_____. Arms and Influence. New Haven: Yale University Press, 1966.

Tercher, Ronald J. The Making of the Test Ban Treaty. The Hague: Nijhoff, 1970.

Tucker, Robert W. A New Isolationism: Threat or Promise? New York: Universe Books, 1972.

VII. The Politics of Foreign Policy

Braestrup, Peter. Big Story: How the American Press and Television Reported and Interpreted the Crisis of Tet 1968 in Vietnam and Washington. Boulder, Col.: Westview Press, 1977, 2 vols.

Fiorina, Morris P. Congress--Keystone of the Washington Establishment. New Haven: Yale University Press, 1977.

Freeland, Richard M. *The Truman Doctrine and the Origins of McCarthyism.* New York: Knopf, 1972.

Frye, Alton. *A Responsible Congress: The Politics of National Security.* New York: McGraw-Hill, 1975.

Hughes, Barry B. *The Domestic Context of American Foreign Policy.* San Francisco: Freeman, 1978.

Kahn, E.J., Jr. *The China Hands: America's Foreign Service Officers and What Befell Them.* New York: Viking, 1975.

Koen, Ross Y. *The China Lobby in American Politics.* New York: Harper and Row, 1974.

McPherson, Harry A. *A Political Education.* Boston: Atlantic (Little, Brown), 1972.

Presthus, Robert. *Elites in the Policy Process.* New York: Cambridge University Press, 1974.

Rieselbach, L.N. *Congressional Politics.* New York: McGraw-Hill, 1972.

Rovere, Richard H., and Arthur M. Schlesinger, Jr. *The MacArthur Controversy and American Foreign Policy.* New York: Farrar, Straus and Girous, 1965.

Rovere, Richard H. *The American Establishment and other Reports, Opinions and Speculations.* New York: Harcourt, Brace and World, 1962.

Russett, Bruce M. and Elizabeth C. Hanson. *Interest and Ideology: The Foreign Policy Beliefs of American Businessmen.* San Francisco: Freeman, 1975.

Sapin, Burton. *The Making of United States Foreign Policy.* New York: Praeger, 1967.

Schandler, Herbert Y. The Unmaking of President Lyndon Johnson and Vietnam. Princeton: Princeton University Press, 1977.

Thomas, John N. The Institute of Pacific Relations: Asian Scholars and American Politics. Seattle: University of Washington Press, 1974.

Tucker, Robert W. The Radical Left and American Foreign Policy. Baltimore: Johns Hopkins Press, 1971.

Wilcox, F.O. Congress, the Executive and Foreign Policy. New York: Harper and Row, 1971.

VIII. U.S. Policy Toward East Asia and the Pacific

Barnett, A. Doak. Communist China and Asia: Challenge to American Policy. New York: Harper and Row, 1960.

Clough, Ralph H. East Asia and U.S. Security. Washington, D.C.: Brookings Institution, 1975.

Dulles, Foster Rhea. American Policy Toward Communist China, 1949-1969. New York: Crowell, 1972.

Dunn, Frederick S. Peace-Making and the Settlement with Japan. Princeton: Princeton University Press, 1963.

Feis, Herbert. The China Tangle: The American Effort in China from Pearl Harbor to the Marshall Mission. Princeton: Princeton University Press, 1953.

Griswold, A. Whitney. The Far Eastern Policy of the United States. New York: Harcourt Brace Jovanovich, 1938.

Hsiao, Gene T. (ed.). *Sino-American Detente and Its Policy Implications*. New York: Praeger, 1974.

Kahn, E.J. *The China Hands: America's Foreign Service Officers and What Befell Them.* New York: Viking, 1975.

Kawai, Kazuo. *Japan's American Interlude*. Chicago: University of Chicago Press, 1960.

McHenry, Donald F. *Micronesia: Trust Betrayed. Altruism vs. Self-Interest in American Foreign Policy.* Washington, D.C.: Carnegie Endowment for International Peace, 1976.

Moreley, James William (ed.). *Prologue of the Future: The United States and Japan in the Postindustrial Age.* Lexington, Mass.: Lexington Books, 1974.

Tsou Tang. *America's Failure in China, 1941-1950.* Chicago: University of Chicago Press, 1963.

U.S. Department of State. *United States Relations with China, with Special Reference to the Period 1944-1949.* (The "China White Paper") Department of State Publication 3573. Washington, D.C.: Department of State, 1949. Stanford, California: Stanford University Press, 1967.

IX. <u>The Indochina War</u>

Austin, Anthony. *The President's War*. Philadelphia: Lippincott, 1971.

Buttinger, Joseph. *Vietnam: A Political History*. New York: Praeger, 1968.

Fall, Bernard B. *Last Reflections on a War*. Garden City, New York: Doubleday, 1967.

_____. The Two Viet-Nams. New York: Praeger, 1967.

_____. Viet-Nam Witness. New York: Praeger, 1966.

Gravel, Mike (ed.). The Pentagon Papers, The Defense Department History of United States Decisionmaking in Vietnam. 4 vols. Boston: Beacon, 1971.

Hersh, Seymour M. Cover-Up. New York: Random House, 1972.

Kraslow, David and Stuart H. Loory. The Secret Search for Peace in Vietnam. New York: Vintage, 1968.

Lake, Anthony (ed.). The Vietnam Legacy: The War, American Society and the Future of American Foreign Policy. New York: New York University Press, 1976.

Mecklin, John. Mission in Torment. Garden City, New York: Doubleday, 1965.

Poole, Peter A. Eight Presidents and Indochina. Huntington, New York: Krieger, 1978.

Porter, Gareth. A Peace Denied: The United States, Vietnam, and the Paris Agreement. Bloomington, Indiana: Indiana University Press, 1976.

Shawcross, William. Sideshow: Kissinger, Nixon and the Destruction of Cambodia. New York: Simon and Schuster, 1979.

X. U.S. Foreign Economic Relations

Baranson, Jack. Technology and the Multinationals. Lexington, Mass.: Lexington Books, 1978.

Bergsten, C. Fred, and Lawrence B. Krause. World Politics and International Economics. Washington, D.C.: Brookings, 1975.

Calleo, D.P., and B. Rowland. America and World Political Economy. Bloomington, Indiana: Inidiana University Press, 1973.

Cohen, Benjamin J. American Foreign Economic Policy. New York: Harper and Row, 1968.

Cohen, Stephen D. The Making of United States International Economic Policy. New York: Praeger, 1977.

El Mallakh, Ragaei and G. McGuire, (eds.). U.S. and World Energy Resources. Boulder, Col.: International Research Centre for Energy and Economic Development, 1978.

Feis, Herbert. The Diplomacy of the Dollar: First Era, 1919-1932. Baltimore: Johns Hopkins Press, 1950.

Friedland, Edward, P. Seabury, and A. Wildavsky. The Great Detente Disaster: Oil and the Decline of American Foreign Policy. New York: Basic Books, 1975.

Gardner, Richard S. Sterling-Dollar Diplomacy. New York: McGraw-Hill, 1969.

Hanrieder, Wolfram F. The United States and Western Europe: Political, Economic and Strategic Perspectives. Cambridge, Mass.: Winthrop, 1974.

Hanson, Simon G. Five Years of the Alliance for Progress. Washington, D.C.: Inter-American Affairs Press, 1967.

Juda, Lawrence. Ocean Space Rights: Developing U.S. Policy. New York: Praeger, 1975.

Szymowycz, Joseph S., and Bard O'Neill. The Energy Crisis and U.S. Foreign Policy. New York: Praeger, 1975.

XI. Surveys of U.S. Foreign Relations

Alexander, Charles C. Holding the Line: The Eisenhower Era, 1952-1961. Bloomington: Indiana University Press, 1975.

Ball, George W. Diplomacy for a Crowded World: An American Foreign Policy. Boston: Atlantic-Little, Brown, 1976.

Bundy, William P. (ed.). Two Hundred Years of American Foreign Policy. New York: New York University Press, 1977.

Bartlett, C.J. The Rise and Fall of Pax Americana: United States Foreign Policy in the Twentieth Century. London: Elek Books, 1974.

Brandon, Henry. The Retreat of American Power. Garden City: Doubleday, 1973.

Chace, James. A World Elsewhere: The New American Foreign Policy. New York: Scribners, 1973.

DeConde, Alexander, (ed.). Encyclopedia of American Foreign Policy. New York: Scribner's, 1978.

Heath, Jim. Decade of Disillusionment: The Kennedy-Johnson Years. Bloomington, Indiana: Indiana University Press, 1975.

Hoffmann, Stanley, Primacy or World Order: American Foreign Policy Since the Cold War. New York: McGraw-Hill, 1978.

Kennan, George. On Dealing with the Communist World. New York: Harper and Row, 1964.

Kissinger, Henry A. American Foreign Policy. Third Edition. New York: Norton, 1977.

Morgan, Roger. The United States and West Germany, 1945-1973. New York: Oxford University Press, 1974.

Nicholas, Harold G. *The United States and Britain*. Chicago: University of Chicago Press, 1975.

Poole, Peter A. *America in World Politics*. New York: Praeger, 1975.

Schaetzel, J. Robert. *The Unhinged Alliance: America and the European Community*. New York: Harper and Row, 1975.

Stern, Laurence. *The Wrong Horse: The Politics of Intervention and Failure of American Diplomacy*. New York: Times Books, 1977.

Szulc, Tad. *The Illusion of Peace: Foreign Policy in the Nixon Years*. New York: Viking, 1978.

Yost, Charles. *The Conduct and Misconduct of Foreign Affairs*. New York: Random House, 1972.